14-Day Wedding Planner With Internet Guide

Don Altman & Sanda Altman

MOON LAKE MEDIA
LOS ANGELES, CA

Copyright © 1999 by Don Altman and Sanda Altman

All rights reserved. No part of this book may be reproduced or transmitted in any form or by any means, electronic or mechanical, including photocopying, recording, or by any information storage or retrieval system—except by a reviewer who may quote brief passages in a review to be printed in a magazine or newspaper—without express written permission from publisher. For information contact: Moon Lake Media, P.O. Box 251466, Los Angeles, CA 90025. Web Site: http://www.moonlakebooks.com

First Printing 1999

While the authors and publisher have done everything possible to cover all aspects of wedding planning, we assume no responsibility or liability for inaccuracies, errors, omissions, inconsistencies, or products and services included herein. Any slights of people or organizations are fully unintentional. When using any of the concepts in this book, and when deciding how to conduct all aspects of weddings and wedding planning, readers must use their own best judgment and consult with wedding coordinators or consultants if necessary.

Publisher's Cataloging-in-Publication
(Provided by Quality Books, Inc.)

Altman, Don, 1950-
    14-day wedding planner with Internet guide : the new, easier way to create your wedding / by Don Altman and Sanda Altman. — 1st ed.
    p. cm.
    Includes index.
    ISBN: 0-9639161-5-7

    1. Weddings—Planning. 2. Weddings—Planning Computer network resources. I. Altman, Sanda. II. Title.

HQ745.A58 1999   392'.5
                                 QBI99-452

Printed in the United States of America

TABLE OF CONTENTS:

Introduction — 1

Chapter 1 — 3
Laying the Best Groundwork
The Special Date • Wedding Calendar • Priorities • Smart Budget Tips & Checklist • Web Tips & Guide

Chapter 2
Letting the Whole World Know — 23
Wedding Party • Guest List • Clergy/Rabbi • Announcements • Unique Sites • Site Planning Tips & Checklist • Web Tips & Guide

Chapter 3
Putting on the Ritz: Shopping in Style — 37
The Perfect Gown • Smart Gown Buying & Renting • Ring Buying • Bridal Registry • Web Tips & Guide

Chapter 4
The Sweet Taste of Good Times — 51
Catering Planning Tips & Checklist • Beverage Budget Secrets • Catering Budget Secrets • Cake Planning Tips & Checklist • Web Tips & Guide

Chapter 5
Setting the Perfect Mood — 63
Invitation Planning Tips & Checklist • Crafting the Ceremony • Music Planning Tips & Checklist • Web Tips & Guide

Chapter 6
Looking Very, Very Good — 77
Photography/Videography Planning Tips & Checklists • Hotel Accommodations • Web Tips & Guide

Chapter 7 87
Flowers & the Perfect Fit
Flower Planning Tips & Checklist • Bridal Bouquet Preservation • Tuxedo Planning Tips & Checklist • Gown Fitting • Web Tips & Guide

Chapter 8 99
Rev Up Your Chariot's Engine
Limousine Planning Tips & Checklist • Marriage License • Prepare/Mail Invitations • Web Tips & Guide

Chapter 9 105
Filling in the Missing Pieces
Head Table • Decorations, Centerpieces & Favors • Reception Checklist • Seating • Web Tips & Guide

Chapter 10 113
Checking in for Facts & Fun
Confirmations • RSVP Count • Honeymoon Trip • Web Tips & Guide

Chapter 11 121
The Personalized Touch
Guest Book & Pen • Attendant Gifts • Web Tips & Guide

Chapter 12 125
Preparing for Things to Come
Rehearsal Dinner Coordination • Pack for the Honeymoon • Web Tips & Guide

Chapter 13 129
Countdown to the Special Day
Miscellaneous • Final Checklist • Web Tips & Guide

Chapter 14 135
Wrapping Up for a New Beginning
Wedding Gown & Bouquet Preservation • Thank You Notes • Web Tips & Guide

Index 139

Introduction

Who Can Use This Book?

Times have changed since our first book, *201 Unique Ways to Make Your Wedding Special* was published. That book, now in a 2nd Edition, helped pioneer and promote the idea of personalized and unique weddings. It has inspired thousands to let their creative spirits take flight, all for the purpose of creating memorable and romantic weddings. Happily, the trend towards personalized weddings is stronger than ever. But to have a dream wedding, you need the time to plan one!

Today, however, there seems to be less and less time available for today's couples or working women. Planning a wedding is no easy task when time is already at a premium. It's no surprise, then, that many of today's brides and grooms-to-be are in need of smart planning help.

When it came time to planning our own wedding, for example, we found ourselves fighting the clock. Our careers and family obligations seemed to absorb every available second, leaving us with little time or energy for all the major wedding decisions we had to make. Out of necessity (and maybe to maintain our sanity), we developed a wedding planning system to give us maximum results from the limited time we had.

The *14-Day Wedding Planner With Internet Guide* is the result of that effort. It's for anyone who feels time-deprived, and who wants their wedding planning experience to be joyful, worry-free, and productive.

Unique Themes for Each Planning Chapter

One thing we discovered while planning our own wedding was that it was easier to do related tasks at the same time. Rather than work from a rigid wedding checklist of disconnected items, *14-Day Wedding Planner With Internet Guide* brings similarly-themed tasks together within a single chapter, or planning "day." Instead of feeling lost and overwhelmed, this will help you stay focused. (Throughout, this book uses the term "you" in the broadest sense, to speak directly to that person, persons, or couple—even friends or family—responsible for bringing the wedding together.)

Staying focused is important, because once you get in the right frame of mind, you bring a sense of continuity, order, and full attention to what you're doing. Since similar tasks are grouped into categories, or themes, *14-Day Wedding Planner With Internet Guide* makes wedding planning more fun, easy, and efficient (Plus, it helps you incorporate the Internet in your planning).

How does this thematic approach work? How will it help you keep your focus and avoid scattering your energy and efforts? For example, Chapter 3, *Putting on the Ritz: Shopping in Style*, brings together key shopping-related tasks. Chapter 5, *Setting the Perfect Mood*, unites important mood enhancing items—from the first impression made by the invitations, to the lasting impression made by the ceremony and the music. Each theme, or category, follows along the basic flow of a wedding calendar. The difference being that the themes help you accomplish your goals with greater purpose and productivity—allowing you to put on your creative hat, spending hat, or whatever "hat" you need for that day. For the first time, you will begin to feel and experience the synergy that your efforts are creating as you plan your special day.

Now, you may be asking: Is it *really* possible to plan a complete, dazzling wedding, including wedding showers, ceremony, reception, out-of-town arrangements, entertainment, photography, and everything else in even short a time? From personal experience, the answer is an unqualified "yes." Let's look at a case study taken from personal experience. Our own wedding, for example, featured a beautiful candle light ceremony under a floral archway, gift baskets for out-of-town guests, separate ceremony and reception sites with live music at both, a sit-down dinner, floral and candle centerpieces, a three-tiered cake decorated with flowers, photography, videography, the longest, stretch-white limousine most of us had ever seen, and much, much more. To top it off, we actually planned the whole wedding in fewer than 14 days of total time. And yes, we used the Internet in certain ways that made the job easier and saved us time.

Our wedding was fun and effortless to plan. Best of all, it went off beautifully, without a hitch. That's one of the reasons that we wanted to share our experiences and write the *14-Day Wedding Planner With Internet Guide.*

Chapter 1

Day 1— Laying the Best Groundwork

You may have heard the phrase, "Rome wasn't built in a day." It points out what many of us know in our hearts: Very little that is *good* is put together haphazardly or without a lot of thought, energy, and dedication. Planning a wedding can sometimes feel overwhelming—especially in the beginning when the entire planning process awaits you. Yet, by following along with the planning stages in this book—chapter-by-chapter—everything eventually gets done.

In fact, you already possess all the tools and skills needed to create the wedding of your dreams. How is this so, you might ask? Anyone with likes, dislikes, tastes, and sensibilities, is ready to make choices based on these judgements and feelings. Let your life's worth of experience guide you in choosing among the many options which will come before you. Stay true to yourself. Trust your feelings. Simply by knowing what you want your wedding to express can transform the planning phase from a chore into a joy.

Just like an architect needs a well-designed blueprint to build a beautiful home, you are the architect and designer of your wedding. As such, this chapter offers checklists, organizational tools, and even unique Web-based aids to help you design your dream wedding and prepare for every contingency, every step of the way.

Select the Special Day

Choosing the date and time for your special day is what starts the wedding wheels rolling. Make sure this day feels right for you—such as astrologically, personally, work-wise, or for whatever reasons you find important. To be on the safe side, make a point of contacting close family and friends to make sure the date and time are available. Once you are satisfied that the date is fine, mark that date on your calendar.

In selecting your wedding day, you may also want to take into account special situations. Suppose, for example, that you have many out-of-town guests and family who also work during the week. In this case, you may find that Saturday is preferable to Sunday because these guests can stay around an extra day, rather than rushing to the airport immediately after the reception.

Once you've identified that special day and time, all else in your wedding calendar will revolve around it. You may be inclined to want to skip ahead, such as wanting to go look for wedding gowns and find wedding sites right away. That's quite all right and acceptable, but don't neglect to lay the groundwork, which is what you're doing in this planning day. Those other, more fun things will come soon enough!

 QUICK NOTES:

- Choose a day that feels right
- Prepare for time off from work
- Check with family and friends to make sure they are available

Smart Wedding Day Planning Tips

You should know, too, that the day and time you choose could have a major impact on your budget. Here's why. Some services and products cost more (or less) on different days. For example, those days and times that are in greatest demand—such as "prime time" Saturday nights—will generally cost more. Afternoon weddings, either Saturday or Sunday, typically cost less because there is less demand—and also because there is reduced alcohol consumption during afternoon weddings.

Holidays are another time that can drive up costs. For example, many couples like to plan Valentine's Day weddings—a time when the cost of flowers—especially roses—can cost two or three times their normal price. In general, you may find that the costs break down as follows:

 SMART BUDGET TIPS:

- High Cost $$$$—Saturday night (prime time)
- Medium Cost $$$—Saturday and Sunday
- Medium-Low Cost $$—Friday night
- Least Cost $—Week night

Start a Wedding Calendar

Wedding Planning can be an organizational nightmare—*unless* you create a system to keep track of the details. This includes everything from appointments with vendors to dates when certain specifics need to be completed—such as mailing out the invitations. Once you get in the habit of keeping everything in order, your job becomes much easier. Best of all, you won't lose phone numbers of vendors, forget about time deadlines, or be unsure about when to schedule a meeting.

Any multi-pocket folder and a large calendar or day-planner should do the job of helping you organize all your wedding records—as will many dedicated wedding planning books that come with pockets for holding notes, estimates, and guest list, etc. If you make your own workbook folder, create separate sections for each of the 20 categories listed below. You might want to add sections for hotel accommodations, bridal registry, the wedding license, and the honeymoon trip. Now, you can look in one place for all your wedding records.

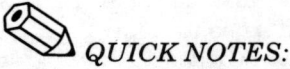 *QUICK NOTES:*

- Create or buy a multi-pocketed organizer
- Keep notes, addresses, phone numbers in your organizer
- Give each of the 20 categories (see below) its own pocket
- Add extra pockets for hotel, registries, wedding license, and honeymoon trip

Determine Priorities

Now that you have a dollar amount that won't break the bank, you will need to decide where to spend that money. Many elements of your wedding will cry out for the best that you can afford. And in truth, there is no small detail. All wedding items are important. Still, you need to prioritize them to give you a sense of what's *really* most vital and meaningful to you.

Use the following 20-point checklist to help determine your priorities. This will let you see where you want to commit your dollars—including those areas where you are willing to spend more, and those where you might be willing to compromise. To help you prioritize, try using one of two methods provided here.

METHOD 1: Give each of the 20 checklist items its own unique ranking—such as writing #1 by the highest priority item, writing #2 by the next priority, and so on through the list down to #20.

METHOD 2: Use a two-part rating system for each item. To do this, simply mark an "X" according to whether a particular item would be nice to have, but not essential, or whether it is an absolute must—such as a designer gown or a Victorian porch ceremony.

PRIORITY-RATING CHECKLIST

	Nice, but Not Essential	Absolutely Must Have	Item Rank #
1) # of Guests ___			
2) # Wedding Party			
3) Ceremony Site			
4) Reception Site			
5) Rings			
6) Gown			
7) Tux			
8) Catering			
9) Beverages			
10) Cake			
11) Invitations			
12) Music			
13) Photography			
14) Videography			
15) Flowers			
16) Centerpiece			
17) Party Favors			
18) Gifts			
19) Dinners			
20) Transportation			

Now that you've prioritized your checklist, do you have a better sense of where you want to allocate those budget dollars? Keep in mind that catering costs are typically one of the most costly parts of a wedding. Later, in Chapter 4, you'll get some tips on how to get the most from the catering budget.

Note that the *Priority-Rating Checklist* is not used for budgeting. You'll use the *Budget Checklist*, with its expanded list of items, to figure the budget.

Smart Planning & Budget Tips

Now that you know your priorities, you need to determine a realistic wedding budget. The budget you create will act as a blueprint for all which follows. It will help set priorities and put your mind at ease in the process. To begin with, let's dispel the myth that you can only have a fantastic wedding on a big budget. And although this book primarily covers planning, it will offer several proven budget tips throughout that will help you get the most out of your wedding dollar.

What does an "average" wedding cost? Estimates from various sources range from between $15-20,000, depending on the region where you live. Of course, it's not uncommon for large, extravagant, highly formal weddings to run well upwards of this average amount. The challenge for most—regardless of who's paying for the wedding—is to create a really special day and still have enough left over to return from the honeymoon relatively debt-free. A smart, realistic budget can help anyone achieve these goals.

The first step is to set your total dollar budget. Is this amount reasonable for the number of guests you want to invite? *Where* you decide to have your wedding can have a large impact on the budget. A backyard reception, for example, will probably cost less than renting out a chic winery as the backdrop for the big day. Basically, though, figure what you can *afford*, then add 10% to that as a contingency amount.

TOTAL BUDGET AMOUNT (with 10% contingency added): _____

Here's an overview of some important budget rules of thumb that will help you every time—whether your wedding costs $5,000 or $50,000. You can use these over and over again, regardless of the "planning day" you're working on. So use them as a guideline whenever you need them.

1) *Set a Realistic Budget*—try to come as close as possible to the budget limit that you really want to commit to the big day. Some information that follows will help you accomplish this goal. A realistic budget will take off some of the pressure and even help you determine priorities.

2) *Plan Ahead*—the more time you have to search for products and services, the more likely you'll find exactly what you're looking for, at a price that's right.

3) *Stay Organized*—this practice will serve you well when things get hectic or you're pressed for time—and sooner or later, they always do! Creating your calendar, you'll not only have more inner peace and calm, but you'll be more likely to make the right decisions.

4) *Remember Your Priorities*—here is one sure way to make your planning and decision-making easier. Determining priorities is essential if you are to have insight into what's most important for you.

5) *Set Your Wedding Style and Theme*—is your wedding going to be ultra-formal, formal, informal, or a small, intimate affair?

   Weddings that feature a particular theme, such as Victorian or Renaissance, often require specially designed and customized items.

   Highly formal weddings may include very large wedding parties, black-tie for all family members, a wedding gown consisting of a long, flowing train, opulent decorations, a full orchestra or band, engraved invitations, and more.

   Formal or semi-formal weddings are less traditional, with fewer bells and whistles, a medium-sized wedding party, and an optional train on the wedding gown—all resulting in a more modest budget.

Informal weddings—which typically numbers fewer than 100 guests—feature the option of more informal clothes for the wedding party, as well as some creative catering options.

Even smaller, *family weddings*—held at a chapel or in the home—may include a handful of close family and friends, with few decorations and dinner at home or in a cozy restaurant. Of course, there are a range of weddings in between all of those just described. Any of the above styles can be done with class and elegance, but finding where yours fits in will certainly help in your planning efforts.

6) *Use Credit Cards*—as a precaution, use credit cards whenever possible. In this way, you are protected by certain consumer protection laws. Use them to put down deposits, and to buy products and services. Contact the Better Business Bureau if you want to know more about the history of a particular company or business.

7) *Ask for Referrals*—you've been to weddings yourself, so ask friends about their experiences with certain wedding vendors. In this way, you might find an excellent vendor, or even avoid a potential wedding nightmare. It's worth asking, and your friends will be more than happy to help.

The Initial Budget

Now it's time to fill in some numbers. The *Budget Checklist* below includes space for three different estimates. Feel free to create as many estimates as are necessary for your particular situation. You might, for example, want to determine how inviting 75, 100, or 125 guests changes the overall budget.

One more thing: Don't expect this initial attempt at an item-by-item budget breakdown to be written in stone. You'll constantly update it as you find out costs in the "real" world and your particular city or region. You might also learn a few things along the way on where to save money, so you can allocate those savings elsewhere—even to a higher priority item. Use this initial budget as a general guideline that will make shopping and procuring all your wedding products and services much, much easier.

BUDGET CHECKLIST

Item	Budget 1 Estimate	Budget 2 Estimate	Budget 3 Estimate
1) # of Guests __			
2) # Wedding Party			
Flower Girl			
Ring Bearer			
3) Ceremony Site			
Location fee			
Clergy fee			
Accessories			
4) Reception Site			
Site Rental			
Accessories			
5) Rings			
6) Gown			
Fitting/Alterations			
Veil/Headpiece/Train			
Shoes/Gloves			
Jewelry/Accessories			
Make-up/Hair			
7) Tux			
Shoes/Tie			
8) Catering			
Hors d'oeuvres			
Main dinner			
9) Beverages			
Bartender			
Corking Fee			

Item	Est. 1	Est. 2	Est. 3
10) Cake			
Cake Cutting			
Addtl. Desserts			
11) Invitations			
Thank You Notes			
Stationery			
Calligraphy			
Postage			
12) Music			
Site			
Cocktail Hour			
Reception			
13) Photography			
Photographer Fee			
Overtime Fee Portraits			
Wedding Album			
Additional Prints			
14) Videography			
Single camera			
2 or 3 Camera Shoot			
Additional Videos			
15) Flowers			
Bridal Bouquet			
Bridesmaid Bouquet			
Corsages			
Boutonnieres			
16) Centerpieces			
Table Decorations			
17) Party Favors			

Item	Est. 1	Est. 2	Est. 3
18) Gifts			
Wedding Party			
Parents			
Out-of-towners			
19) Dinners			
Rehearsal			
Additional			
20) Transportation			
Limousine			
Guest Trans/Parking			
TOTALS			

For those who have a computer, you can create your budget using a spreadsheet program, such as *Quicken* or *Excel*. This will enable you to update it easily, as well as assign percentages to particular items. If you assign percentages, you can simply enter a total budget dollar amount and have the entire budget automatically figured for you. In a moment, you'll learn how to do this on a wedding Web site.

 **DAY 1—WEB TIPS & RESOURCE GUIDE**

Thanks to a variety of useful Web tools, a new couple can budget their wedding, create and share a Wedding Calendar or to-do list, and even use the Web to prepare for their financial future. It's all available, on any Web desktop. The tools mentioned here are free. All that's required, in most cases, is to register at the Web site. Throughout the *14-Day Wedding Planner With Internet Guide,* we'll mention such specialized sites.

In addition to specialized sites are more general, all-purpose wedding Web sites. Such all-purpose sites are ideal for locating most things relating to weddings, including a list of vendors, bridal registries, etiquette tips, and even musical selections. The Internet contains many all-purpose wedding Web sites. Each offers something a little different, and the listings that follow each chapter will describe some of their features.

Budgeting Online

TheKnot.com is one of the Web's most popular wedding sites. In fact, the number of people visiting The Knot on a monthly basis has grown as large as the circulation of the wedding industry's two biggest magazine publications—combined. This site's Big Day Budgeter allows you to get a complete budget, customized for those items you want, in just minutes.

The Knot's "Big Day Budgeter" is located at:

http://www.theknot.com/budgetermain.html

The budgeter is easy-to-follow. It's ideal for first-timers who know nothing about spreadsheets or budgeting. You simply enter the budget dollars, the number of guests, and the number in the wedding party. Then, choose the *Update Budget* button. In less time than it takes to walk down the aisle, you'll have a complete wedding budget estimate! Every major category is provided. However, you can get a more accurate budget if you go through the Big Day Budgeter and choose only those items that apply to your wedding. For example—if your wedding does not include videography, then you leave that category unchecked.

The Knot's Big Day Budgeter applies percentages to each item on the list. That percentage, however, does not take into account your priorities. Still, it's a good way to get started, and it can show you in an instant how your dollars will be distributed depending on the number of guests you have. Once you get your budget, simply print it out. It will also be saved under your name after you register on The Knot's web site. You can fill in your own, real budget dollars in the space provided, and get an instant, updated total anytime you want.

On the next page is an example of a Big Day Budgeter that we filled out:

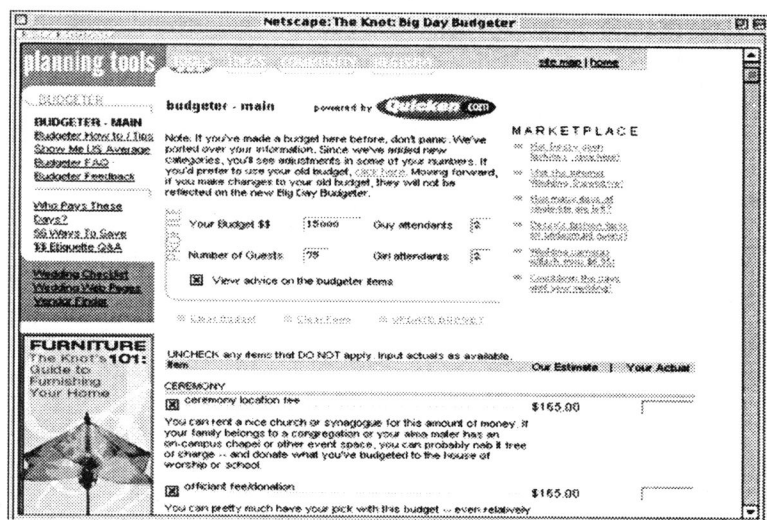

Here's another way to do budgeting on the Web. If you have your own spreadsheet program, such as *Excel*, you can make an html version (that's Web-speak for the language that makes a Web page) of an *Excel* spreadsheet with all your wedding calculations included. You can publish the *Excel* worksheet on a personal wedding web page, or store the *Excel* file online at one of the Web calendar or virtual desk locations that follow. Once it's safely stored, you and your partner can retrieve it to make additions or changes as required. Or, you can simply e-mail the budget file to each other.

Financial Tools Online

One Web site, hosted by the accounting software company *Quicken*, offers a collection of helpful financial-oriented wedding information, including a "Life Events Planner."

Quicken's Life Events Planner is located at:

http://www.quicken.com/life_events/wedding

At the *Quicken* site you will find a host of valuable tips, such as how a joint name will effect the holding of assets, how-to financially set up and manage your new household, and how to prepare for a new family. In addition, this site contains links to other wedding sites and articles.

Calendars & Organizers Online

How would you like to have a *free* online calendar that contains all your wedding planning information, addresses, to-do lists, *and* could be shared with your partner for updating and making appointments? If this sounds too good to be true, it's not. These tools all exist. Plus, they don't take up any of your hard drive space and require only a Web browser (such as *Netscape Navigator* or *Internet Explorer*) to use them.

These Web tools may be particularly useful if either the bride or groom-to-be work out-of-town or are mobile much of the time. A shared calendar lets one or both partners make calendar updates and prepare for upcoming appointments. This also saves time and avoids conflicts by showing each person's current availability—thus making it easier to schedule meetings and appointments with caterers, florists, and others.

More and more applications and capabilities are being offered online to attract users. Web calendars and organizers make it easy to create to-do lists, schedule meetings and tasks, and even broadcast e-mails and updates friends and family. Some Web calendars let the user publish a calendar Web page so anyone you want can access it. This is ideal for announcing the time and location of showers, bachelor parties, the rehearsal dinner, wedding ceremony and reception information, and much more. This can expand this into a family calendar, with dates of birthdays and anniversaries.

The two following Web calendar sites are full-featured. They offer integrated e-mail, calendar, sharing of files and photos, a daily planner, and even browser bookmarks.

Visto Corporation's Web calendar is located at:

http://www.visto.com

Visto offers password protection for files and calendars so no unauthorized persons can gain access to any of your wedding planning details.

Another useful Web calendar, from *Magically, Inc.*, can be located at:

http://www.magicaldesk.com

Both the Visto and Magically Web calendars can even synchronize files between computers. This means that the latest, most up-to-date wedding information and planning notes can be shared by whoever is involved in helping plan the wedding. What's more, such "group" planning information can be accessed at work, home, or on the road. So, regardless of where you or your partner are physically located, you can always retrieve vital files. Plus, these calendars are compatible with the popular *Lotus* "Organizer" and *Microsoft* "Outlook" personal inventory manager programs.

Sharing your wedding files and calendar is now as easy as designating which files you want to make available, and to whom. If a particular wedding vendor is computer-savvy, you can include them in your "group" list of those whose calendars you can view in order to schedule appointments or communications.

Several Web calendars are available online. If you want to find more, go to one of the search engines like *Yahoo.com*, *Lycos.com*, or *Excite.com*, and type in the word "Calendar" which is likely to bring up several names, including some of the additional Web calendars mentioned here:

http://www.scheduleonline.com
http://www.when.com
http://www.jump.com
http://www.calendar.yahoo.com
http://www.pacificawebcal.net

General, All-purpose Wedding Sites Online

All-purpose wedding Web sites offer a wide range of services. Familiarize yourself with them, because they'll come in handy throughout the planning process, whether looking for a gown, signing up for a bridal registry, or making announcements. Here is a preview of some sites that offer solid features. The Web site from *Modern Bride Magazine* is located at:

http://www.modernbride.com

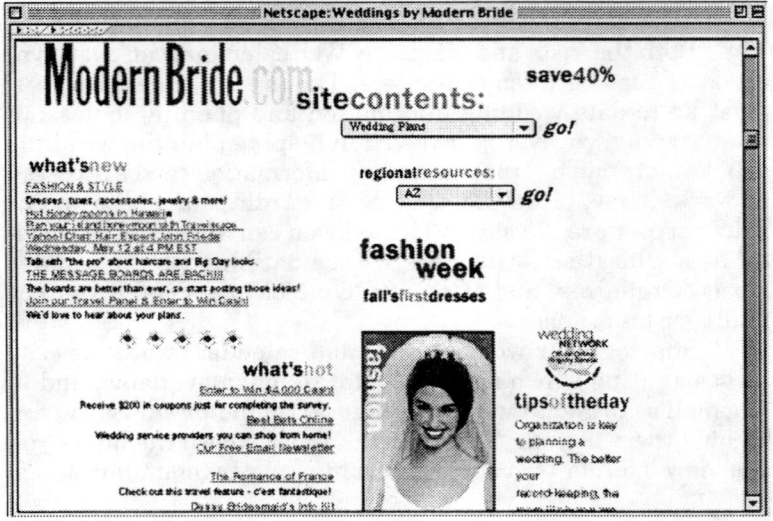

The Wedding Channel Web site is sophisticated and well-designed. It lets the user create a custom wedding Web page—allowing you to choose the background, a photo, text color, and add a personal profile. Once the custom wedding web page is created, announcements are e-mailed from the site. How long does it take to create a personalized wedding Web page? We did it in about 15 minutes.

http://www.weddingchannel.com

The Knot, the popular wedding Web site mentioned earlier, is a full-featured site with lots of guidance and ideas regarding etiquette, checklists, and budgeting. One of its best features is access to over 100 wedding designers and 8000 different gowns.

http://www.theknot.com

(see picture on next page)

The Ultimate Wedding Web site is another full-featured site that offers all major wedding services to users, including an extensive links area at *weddinglinksgalore.com*.

http://www.ultimatewedding.com

The Mining Company Web site isn't a Wedding site, but actually a guide to help search out other useful wedding sites on the Internet. This informative Web site features a wide range of articles on almost every wedding topic.

http://weddings.miningco.com

There are many other all-purpose wedding Web sites that are worth checking out. If you don't find what you're looking for, use the Web search engines to find others. In the chapters that follow, we'll discuss how to use the Web to find resources close to your home. For now, here are some additional full-featured wedding Web sites:

http://www.abridesbestfriend.com/
http://www.wedding-world.com
http://www.weddingweb.com
http://www.bridesandgrooms.com
http://www.weddinglinksgalore.com
http://www.brideworld.com
www.bridalsonline.com
http://www.wedding-world.com
http://www.wednet.com
http://www.weddingelement.com

Etiquette Advice Online

Sooner or later, you may find yourself having to answer a difficult question regarding etiquette. Don't worry—the Web offers a wealth of sources for resolving matters of etiquette.

You can find some etiquette-oriented sites at the following Web addresses:

http://www.wednet.com/questions/default.asp
http://weddings.miningco.com
http://www.theknot.com/askcarley.html

In Summary

You now have a good idea of how to budget according to your priorities, create a calendar, and make a wedding organizer. If your exact budget is still a work in progress, that's okay. The numbers will change as you discover that you can save a little bit here and a little bit there. Keep refining the budget as you go, always keeping your priorities in mind. You are now familiar with several Web wedding sites, calendars, and other tools. Maybe you have already done an online budget and put up a free wedding Web page at one of the suggested sites. So what's next?

Some time between now and the next chapter, try thinking about the following things: What kind of setting do you want for your special day—a view over the ocean? A view from a vineyard? A favorite church or chapel? Also, start thinking about your guest list, and start jotting down names whenever you have some free time. Finally, consider what the ideal marriage ceremony will be like.

If you find your mind running ahead to other things or ideas you may have—even if these are not related to the current or next week's planning—jot them down and place them in the proper sleeve of your personal wedding folder or organizer.

Planning the budget is a lot of work. It takes lots of energy and effort to create something beautiful and enduring. By completing the budget you have now taken a big step forward, with many more to come. But it will all be worth it, when in the next planning day you'll begin to make the dream a reality by *letting the whole world know* about your upcoming wedding.

Chapter 2

Day 2— Letting the Whole World Know

Do you remember the look on the faces of the those you first told about your upcoming wedding? Almost everyone smiles when they hear the good news. There's an unbridled optimism, and a sense of hope and joy that surrounds the union of a man and woman. Don't be shy about letting others know, because more than likely, you are brightening their day. In this chapter, or planning day, our theme of *letting the whole world know* will include several different ways of spreading the word. We hope that you enjoy each and every one.

Choose the Wedding Party

Don't wait too long to ask friends and family to participate as members of your wedding party. Make a point of doing this as soon as you fix the wedding date—just in case you need to find an alternate. The maid of honor and best man hold significant places in any wedding. They hold the rings (of the groom and bride, respectively), make toasts, and assist in handling many prior and wedding-day details. Their help is often invaluable.

In addition to the maid of honor and best man, how many bridesmaids and ushers will grace your special day? That all depends on your wedding traditions and customs, and how many guests will be attending. Usually, the larger the affair, the larger the wedding party. One general rule regarding your choice is this: Choose those who are closest and dearest to you. They are your honored guests, yet they must be willing and able to participate fully, as needed.

While most attendants pay for their own transportation and clothing, be sensitive to those for whom this is a hardship. If necessary, the bride and groom or other family members can help with these costs. All members of the wedding party should be invited to the rehearsal dinner, showers, bachelor parties, and other meaningful events.

For some weddings, one or more flower girls and a ring bearer add a touch of charm that rounds off the wedding party. Other friends can play a role as well—such as helping with last minute coordination. One way to avoid confusion and keep everyone happy is to make a list of responsibilities for each person involved.

 QUICK NOTES:

- Get your wedding party in place as soon as you set a wedding date
- The number of attendants will depend on the number of guests and traditions
- Invite all wedding party members to all important events
- Let everyone know exactly what details he or she will be responsible for, like holding rings, making toasts, etc.
- Avoid confusion by writing up a list of responsibilities

Create a Guest List

In order to plan your wedding, you need to know how many people will be invited—50, 100, or 300? You may be surprised how the number magically seems to grow and grow. Try to get as close as possible to a number that you can settle on. In some cases, your choice of a ceremony or reception site will depend on the number of guests you invite. If you can't determine this with any exactness, try to get within 10% of the number of expected guests. This should at least help identify those sites that can accommodate your requirements.

Making the guest list can be difficult. It's not unusual for there to be a difference of opinion on who to invite. Be patient and respectful of each other's opinions. Most importantly, try to compromise. Give yourself enough time between creating the guest list and mailing out invitations for adding or changing the list.

Don't be afraid to seek etiquette advice. Should you invite children? Should you let bridal party members bring dates? Should the minister, clergy, or rabbi bring his or her spouse? Sometimes the answers to these questions depend on your relationship with those involved. Yes, this area of wedding planning can be a balancing act, but you will do fine as long as you remember to be keep your cool—*and* check your address book and e-mail for names of people you may have overlooked.

 QUICK NOTES:

- Try to get within 10% of the number of expected guests
- Give yourself enough time for adding or changing your list
- Compromise and be patient
- Don't be afraid to seek etiquette advice
- Check your e-mail and day-planner for names of people you may have overlooked

Contact the Clergy, Rabbi, or Officiator

If you are affiliated with a particular church or synagogue, you may want to schedule the ceremony there. Because you are a member, you will may receive a special rate, or only be required to pay for the staff—with no charge for the site rental. Even if you're not a member of a particular institution, you may still be able to get married there—but you may need sponsorship from someone who is already a member.

Regardless of where you get married, you should meet with the officiator in advance. Ideally, you want to find someone who shares your feelings about what the ceremony will be like. The more you develop a special relationship with your officiator, the more your wedding ceremony will express the love, respect, and feelings you want to share.

Do you want to take a role in shaping your ceremony? Will your officiator agree to this? If you're not sure, ask. Some religious or traditional ceremonies are straightforward and leave little room for personalization. Others encourage the couple to include personal information into the ceremony.

 QUICK NOTES:

- Members of a church or synagogue usually receive special rates, such as paying for staff only
- Non-members can be sponsored through current members
- Get to know the clergy, rabbi, or officiator
- Find out what role, if any, you can take in shaping the ceremony

Make Announcements

There are many ways to make wedding announcements. There are intimate ways to get the news of the engagement to family and friends—and there are formal approaches. Let's start with family and friends. One way to break the news is by having a no-gift engagement party which can be given by either set of parents, or by the couple themselves. If you want, send out invitations announcing your engagement and the party. Or, you may decide to be more informal and call, or even use e-mail—we'll illustrate how to send e-mail announcements in the *Web Tips & Resource Guide* at the end of the chapter. Either way, a party provides a nice, comfortable setting for families to get acquainted.

A more traditional way to make announcements is through a couple's hometown newspaper—as well as the newspaper in the city where the parents reside. Each daily paper is different. The best way to find out how to send in an announcement is to call and ask to speak with the editor in charge of this. Information may be taken over the phone or mailed in. Typically, announcements aren't published until perhaps shortly before the wedding—from eight to twelve weeks. But you can prepare the announcement and have it ready to go when the time comes.

Before calling any publication, first look at engagement announcements in the newspaper where you'd like to be included. This will give you a good idea of what that publication is looking for and how to write your own announcement. Always make it legible—typewritten if possible. In some cases, you may be able to send in a black and white glossy photo for printing.

Here's one final, but important point. When announcing for an engagement party, the question of bridal registry plans inevitably arises. For this reason, it helps to know where you will be registering before making your announcements. In fact, we'll be getting to that phase of planning in the next chapter.

 QUICK NOTES:

- Send out invitations or contact family and friends by phone or e-mail
- Contact local newspaper for announcement policy and requirements
- Use existing newspaper announcements as a guide to write your own
- Publish newspaper announcements 8 to 12 weeks before the wedding
- Coordinate your informal announcement with the completion of bridal registry

Non-Denominational Ceremony Sites

Some couples prefer to have a non-denominational wedding—and there are many charming non-denominational chapels that perform this service. Find out what's included, as some offer complete packages—including the officiator, flowers, and music—while others may require that you bring your own minister, decorations, and musicians. Be sure to add ceremony accessories such as a ring pillow, candles, wine glasses, and canopies to your budget.

 QUICK NOTES:

- Find out what's included with non-denominational chapels, such as the officiant's fee, music, and flowers
- Add ceremony accessories like candles, wine glasses, ring pillow, etc., into the budget
- Put down a deposit and secure the site as soon as you find the right one

Unique Reception Sites

Finding the perfect ceremony and reception site are critical to setting the mood, tone, and spirit of your wedding. While you want to find the perfect site, keep in mind that the really good sites are in great demand. This is especially true if your wedding is scheduled during the height of the wedding season. In some cases, you may need to reserve a site a year or more in advance. So, as a rule of thumb, the quicker you find a site, the better.

Is there a truly unique site to match your wedding? A cornucopia of sites exist for every taste and style. Here's where your imagination and vision can soar. Consider, for example, that you can get married in almost any conceivable place—well, except maybe the White House. But you *can* get married at some Presidential Museums and famous historical sites. The *National Register of Historical Places* lists historical landmarks and sites across the nation.

Museums and art galleries, too, can provide a stunning setting for a wedding. One museum in California, for example—the Kellogg House—offers an authentic Victorian setting. Don't forget your local city, county, or state park system. They often maintain beautiful wedding sites consisting of rose gardens, parks overlooking the ocean, and beautiful community centers. Some cities, such as Los Angeles, even have a wedding consultant on staff. Call your local Department of Parks, local Chamber of Commerce, or Historical Society for a list of available sites.

When planning for an outdoor wedding, check into local requirements, such as an outdoor wedding permit, associated fees, and off-site catering availability. Also, inquire into rental costs for necessities like tents, tables, chairs, and even heat lamps. If you're planning on including alcoholic beverages, be sure to ask if this is permitted—some community sites do not permit alcohol of any kind, not even wine.

Depending on the reception site, there are some other arrangements you may need to provide for, such as ceremony and catering seating diagrams, parking, and site access for wedding vendors.

 QUICK NOTES:

- Secure ceremony and reception sites far in advance
- For unique locations, consider museums and historical landmarks
- Obtain a list of wedding sites from the local city, state, county Department of Parks, Chamber of Commerce, and Historical Society
- Always check for permits, rentals, availability of off-site catering and alcoholic beverages (even wine)
- Prepare seating charts for ceremony and reception, arrange for parking and site access for other vendors

Reception Site Planning

Ultimately, your dream site search will be aided greatly if you know what you're looking for in advance. Wine lovers might want a wedding at a winery, while lovers of the out-of-doors might want a wedding overlooking the ocean. However, if you're considering a lot of different sites, you may not be able to visit them all in one day. So ask the wedding coordinator at each to send you photos and other information about the site in question. This will help narrow the field and save you time.

If you're really serious about a particular site, ask about the catering specifics (see Chapter 4). You need to ask about kitchen facilities and the potential for off-site catering when checking out reception sites. Above all, personally visit any site you are considering. Once you determine the site, don't waste any time in putting down a deposit and securing it for your wedding. If your ceremony and reception sites are different, then allow for enough time to travel between them.

Take along a copy of the following checklist when meeting with site coordinators or managers. Always ask for a written quote covering all the details for which there are charges. You can compare these with any other estimates you may obtain.

 SITE CHECKLIST

FEES & POLICIES
- Amount of Deposit needed to secure reservation
- Postponement/Cancellation Policy
- Final Payment Due Date
- Rental Fees
- Parking Fees
- Arrival/Departure Time & Overtime Fees
- Contract
- Off-site catering regulations
- Outdoor Permits & Fees
- Restrictions
- Clean Up/Security Deposit
- Gratuities/Sales Tax
- Liability Insurance

FACILITIES
- Seating Capacity
- Coat Check
- Type of catering: On-site or Off-site
- Kitchen Facilities
- Microphone/Speaker System
- Music/Dancing Facilities
- Bar Facilities
- Alcohol: Yes/No
- Smoking: Yes/No
- Candles: Yes/No
- Decoration Guidelines
- Separate Bridal Room
- Receiving Line Area
- Chairs, Linens, Tableware, Centerpieces
- Parking

Smart Reception Planning & Budget Tips

Here's a reception site idea that may help the budget: Restaurants that specialize in weddings—depending on size and availability, of course. Many restaurants feature a full bar, and you may even be able to use the entire restaurant for the wedding. Usually, restaurants do not charge site fees or other rentals. They may already have centerpieces or floral arrangements for the tables. Most importantly, if the restaurant is one of your favorite places, you know that the food is going to be excellent.

 **DAY 2—WEB TIPS & RESOURCE GUIDE**

Announcements Online

Thanks to the magic of the Internet, anyone can create a personal announcement page and send e-mail announcements to multiple recipients. One advantage of this method is that announcement and registry information can be provided simultaneously. That's because many Internet or online announcements are linked to a bridal registry. Anyone who visits your personal announcement or wedding page can instantly look at your bridal registry selections. And, these services are free.

One free announcement service, WedNet, places your name and wedding date on a master announcement page with other couples. Visitors simply search by the date of the wedding, or by the name of bride or the groom. Once located, visitors can browse your private wedding page filled with details about where and when you are getting married.

http://www.wednet.com/announce

WeddingElement lets you broadcast an engagement message via e-mail to several people at once. Most wedding Web sites offer this capability.

http://weddingelement.com/announcments

TheKnot lets you create a personal wedding page from which to announce your engagement in style—by including an engagement photo and even a short description of your first meeting.

http://www.theknot.com/pwp.html

(see picture on next page)

32

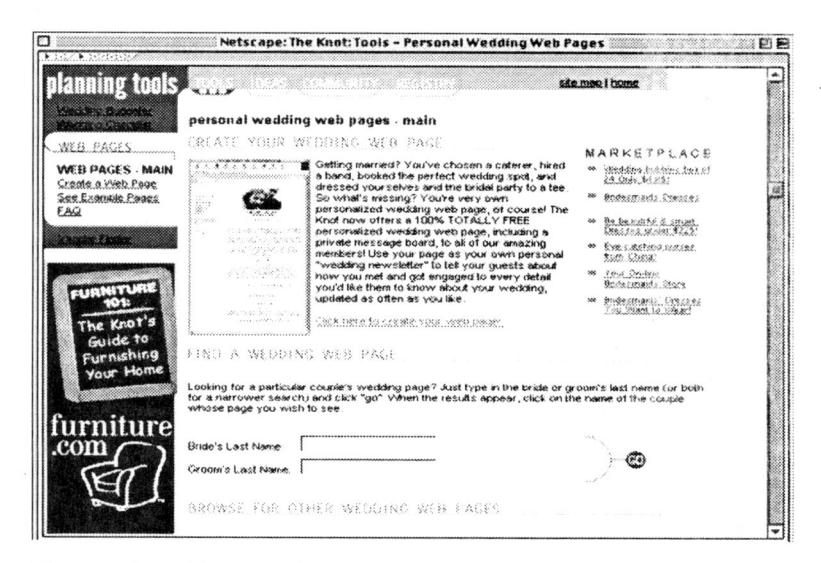

Reception Sites Online

There are several ways of obtaining information on the Web. One method, involves typing a word or phrase into the "search" field of *Yahoo.com*, *Excite.com*, *Lycos.com*, or other Web search engines. However, there's another excellent method for finding business oriented services and products in your neighborhood. It's the Web version of the Yellow Pages. In fact, it's even called the Yellow Pages. Each search engine has a version online, usually accessible from the search engine's Home Page, or main page.

Suppose you want to find a local wedding reception site. Yahoo's Yellow Pages can take you there. First, go to the correct Yahoo page as listed below. Next, key in your local address or city. Then type in the service you're looking for, such as "wedding sites." The results even tell how many miles the establishment is located from you. Use this time saver for most products and services, and you may be surprised at how useful it is.

http://yp.yahoo.com

(see picture on next page)

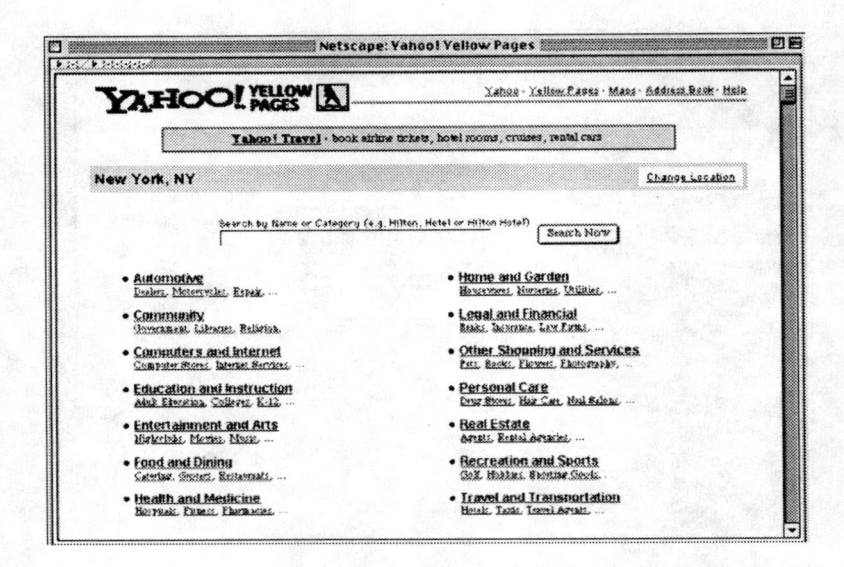

Of course, many all-purpose wedding Web sites offer vendor information. To find vendors through Wedding-World's site, you choose your local state and narrow down your search from there.

http://wedding-world.com/receptionsites.html

Another useful way to find sites is through the local Chamber of Commerce. The site shown here lists thousands of cities and Chambers of Commerce from around the world. Here is an quick and easy way to obtain city information on sites, tours, and more.

http://chamber-of-commerce.com/exe/search

(see picture on next page)

In Summary

By the time you've finished this planning day, you've accomplished a tremendous amount. The news of your special day is making buzzing along pathways leading to your closest friends and family. It may be circling through cyberspace! At this point, you may have heard back from your wedding party, and you will undoubtedly be in touch more often as your wedding day approaches. Hopefully, you have been able to find a ceremony and reception site that match your dreams. After all this preparation, it's time for some fun. That's why the next planning "day" is all about *shopping in style*.

Chapter 3

Day 3— Putting on the Ritz: Shopping in Style

Chances are that the bride and groom-to-be have been looking at bridal attire by now. Well, at least *she* has. Gowns are usually high up on the priority list. So if you have already looked for gowns or know what design, style, or look appeals to you, so much the better—you're ahead of the pace.

Even though this book is organized by "days," don't feel pressured to find your gown on one particular day. This is one time you'll want to be absolutely sure you've made the right choice. By doing your research in advance, however, you might find that perfect gown sooner than you think.

If your wedding is one year away, then you can browse gowns at a more leisurely pace. But if your wedding is fewer than six months away, then you'll need to get started. That's because getting the gown size you want can take from three to six months. The reason? Some manufacturers or designers wait for a large number of orders come in before they start to sew a particular gown. This doesn't mean you *can't* find a gown quickly. As you'll soon discover, there are many ways to find gowns.

That said, let's remember that this chapter is about realizing your dream and getting to imagine more vividly than ever what your special day will be like. Enjoy every moment of it.

Finding the Perfect Gown

For many brides, the gown symbolizes the once-upon-a-time fairy-tale charm and uniqueness of the wedding day. First, however, you need to do a little preparation that will ensure a perfect fit—such as buying the wedding lingerie and shoes necessary for sizing. Also, you'll want to keep an eye out for all the bridal accessories at this same time, including a handbag, gloves, veil, stockings, earrings, and jewelry. Lastly, bear in mind the season when your wedding will occur, as well as the theme and colors, since these will influence your choice of gown.

QUICK NOTES:

- Buy wedding-day lingerie, and anything necessary for sizing gown
- Be on the lookout for accessories like gloves, handbag, jewelry, earrings, etc.
- Keep in mind your wedding theme and colors

Fortunately, there are more ways than ever before to shop for gowns, to find the right gown, and to get gowns in all price ranges. Bridal magazines have long been a useful way to check out designs and styles before going shopping. Today, many manufacturers and designers have Web sites where the new season's gowns can be viewed. This convenient method of finding gowns will be covered in detail at the end of the chapter, in the *Web Tips & Resource Guide*.

Depending on the priority you've set for the gown, you have two basic choices: To buy or rent. Either method can result in an extraordinary gown to match your wedding day dreams. First, let's look at the option of buying a gown.

Smart Gown Buying

There are several kinds of gown you can purchase, and these fall into the following basic categories:

- Designer Gown
- Ready-to-Wear
- Custom-Designed Gown
- Previously Purchased Gown (New & Used)
- Vintage & Antique Gown
- Heirloom Gown

Let's take a closer look at each of these options. High fashion designer gowns can be the height of beauty and elegance. They also tend to be more expensive. There's also the concern of how long these gowns will take to get made and delivered. How can you ensure that your designer gown will arrive on-time? Have the salon write down a delivery date in writing. Ideally, this should be delivered to you about 6 to 8 weeks prior to the wedding.

You may be fortunate to find your exact gown in the size you want at a local bridal salon. However, always get the cost of fitting and alterations in writing. After all, you really want to pay for the gown, not for hidden alteration costs. And, don't forget to ask for a copy of all the original measurements taken at the time of the sizing—this way there can be no dispute if the gown doesn't fit and you ask the salon to resize you.

Another option? You might want to consider having a personal buying service, such as *Discount Bridal Service*, or DBS, work on your behalf. A well-known, established company, DBS offers a nationwide network of independent bridal consultants who work out of their home, reducing overhead. Nationally advertised gowns are purchased in volume through a central office. The good news is that the savings are passed down to the buyer, usually amounting to a discount of between 20-40%. DBS carries most major designers and manufacturers, with gowns usually delivered from 8 to 24 weeks after placing an order. Plus, DBS representatives are trained to size gowns according to each designer's measurement charts. (Wedding gown sizes do not necessarily correspond to common dress sizes, which is why you need someone who knows the manufacturer's sizing system.) DBS can be located though the Yellow Pages, and on the Web (of course!).

What about ready-to-wear gowns? Many welknown designers sell through nationwide retail stores where you can purchase their gowns "off-the-rack." One big advantage here is that you can save a lot of time, and you won't experience a long wait for your gown. The fitting is typically done at the store, and you'll know what extra alteration charges there are, if any. In addition, many major department stores include a bridal gown department. As well as being affordable, some ready-to-wear stores offer another feature—if you don't live near a store, you can often shop from a catalogue or over the phone.

A custom-designed gown may seem expensive and extravagant, but it doesn't have to be. The key is finding a referral for someone who can sew a fabulous gown to order. First, eliminate guesswork by showing pictures of what you want your gown to look like. If you're having a seamstress make you a custom gown, don't wait until the last minute. Be prepared to spend some extra time fitting and refitting the gown until everything is perfect.

Many brides don't know that consignment stores sometimes carry never worn designer gowns, with savings of up to 50%, as well as antique or vintage gowns. If you can, try to find a consignment or second hand store that specializes in gowns. With some luck, you may find a quality new or vintage gown for a lot less money.

Lastly, you may be fortunate enough to find an heirloom gown among your family's treasures. Another place to look? Search the classifieds for antique or heirloom gowns. And be sure to figure in the cost of cleaning and fitting this kind of gown into your budget.

Whatever the source for buying your gown, never pay more than 50% deposit beforehand—preferably on a credit card. You should get written confirmation of the delivery date on your order, and you can schedule a fitting at the same time.

QUICK NOTES:

- Personal buying services like *Discount Bridal Service* can save 20-40%
- Buying ready-to-wear from designer or department stores saves time
- Get cost of alterations in advance, and in writing
- Get a copy of sizing measurements in case of a fitting problem later on
- Get referrals and leave a lot of extra time for hand-sewn gowns
- Search consignment and second hand shops for never before worn gowns, as well as antique or vintage gowns.
- Use the classified to find heirloom or antique gowns
- Confirm gown delivery in writing, and schedule fitting date

Smart Gown Renting

There are many bridal rental shops located in most major, and many smaller cities. You may pay a premium to rent a designer gown, but probably a lot less than the cost of owning that same gown. Another advantage of renting is that it is convenient and eliminates waiting for a gown.

QUICK NOTES:

- Find bridal gown rental shops in local phone book
- Wear a designer gown at a reduced cost
- Even for rentals, confirm the delivery and fitting dates in writing

Shopping for Rings

Some of us shop for wedding rings without really knowing much about the value of diamonds, gold, and jewelry design. For this reason alone, it pays to shop several stores when looking for wedding bands and engagement rings. There are numerous nationwide jewelry chains and other local merchants who are willing to guarantee your jewelry's value in writing. You can also get an independent appraisal for the jewelry after the purchase. Here's another reason why using credit cards acts as valuable protection.

Don't be intimidated when purchasing rings. Do your homework and compare, and you'll find this to be an enjoyable part of your wedding journey. If you happen to have some old jewelry, for example, you may be able to trade it in and get the value of the gold towards your new purchase.

QUICK NOTES:

- Compare prices from several jewelers and national chains
- Use your credit card for the ring purchase
- Trade in your unused gold jewelry to be credited against your purchase
- For extra security, obtain a written appraisal

Bridal Registry

This is always fun. You get to romp around your favorite stores saying, "I want this, and this, and that!" This is an activity that both the bride and groom-to-be will want to do together. Choose your stores in advance, then go and register. To make things easier, make a list of what you really need. Register for these first, then let your imagination go wild and roam through those departments that feel most important.

How many stores should you register in? You may want to limit it to no more than two, possibly three, unless you're not concerned about receiving incomplete sets of silver and dinnerware. You may also want to consider registering in a store that allows for refunds as well as exchanges. Make sure you ask about their registry policy. Finally, try to make a point of registering for gifts in various price ranges, which will be helpful to your guests.

QUICK NOTES:

- Make a list of most-needed items before going to register
- Register in two, maybe three stores at most to avoid getting incomplete sets of table and dinnerware
- If possible, register in a store that allows both refunds and exchanges
- Include a wide pricing range for registry items

DAY 3—WEB TIPS & RESOURCE GUIDE

Gowns Online

It's really amazing how much the Web can help in finding the perfect gown. The benefit of shopping this way is that almost any gown and designer can be located—and you never have to leave the comfort of home. While you can look at thousands of designs, you will still want to try on the real thing before buying. None-the-less, the Web offers a time-saving method of shopping for gowns that is hard to beat. Basically, you can find gowns on the Web by using one of the four following methods:

1) Enter the words "wedding gowns" into your favorite search engine to find everything including designers like Bill Levkoff and Janell Berté, wedding kimonos from Japan, and imported, vintage and custom-made creations.
2) Locate your favorite wedding designer's Web site and gain information on where to find retail outlets near your home.
3) Use the online Yellow Pages to search for "Bridal Gowns" or "Weddings" to find bridal salons or designer outlets in your neighborhood.

4) Check the all-purpose wedding Web sites to find fairly complete bridal gown offerings that may help you—and your bridal party—dress to impress.

TheKnot.com wedding web site features an extensive list over 100 designers and 8000 different gowns—searchable by designer, style, or by store location.

http://www.theknot.com

BridalsOnline.com offers only current season gowns from many well-known designers—at a discounted price.

http://www.bridalsonline.com

UltimateWedding.com offers discounts, but has a smaller gown collection. Keep in mind that each wedding Web site may have a slightly different collection. UltimateWedding, for example, carried Jessica McClintock, while some others did not.

http://www.ultimatewedding.com

TNCWeddings.com is a Web site by Town and Country magazine. It offers a geographic wedding vendor search capability, with an especially nice feature that allows for viewing gowns full length, both from the front and the back. Over 30 designers are represented.

http://www.tncweddings.com

Discount Bridal Service, mentioned earlier in this chapter, offers a Web site which links to over 40 bridal manufacturers, for both gowns and bridesmaids dresses. DBS also conveniently links to the WeddingChannel gown search.

http://www.discountbridalservice.com

SecondHand.com is an Internet Resale Directory that's ideal if you're looking for vintage, antique, or previously purchased gowns. Over 40,000 stores—all kinds of second hand, thrift, and antique stores—are listed in their directory.

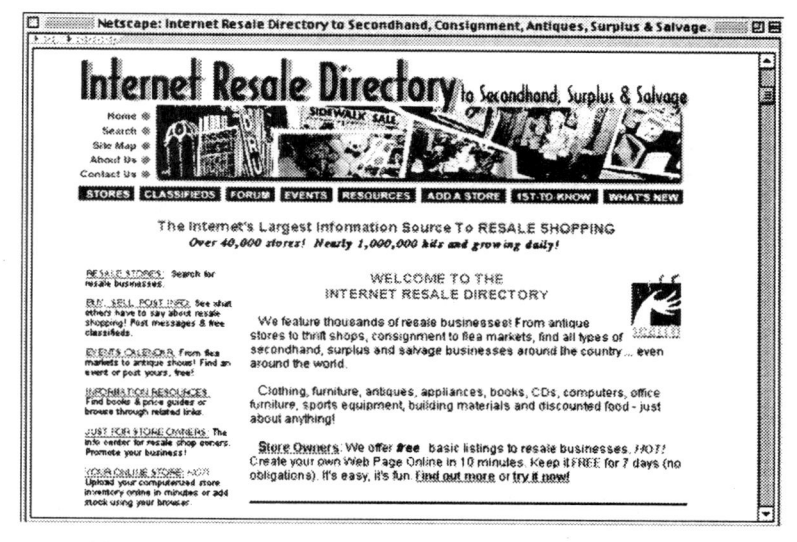

http://www.secondhand.com

Two more sources for finding gowns by geographical location are found at the following Web sites:

http://wedding-world.com/gowns.html
http://www.wedfind.com/fstatecity.cfm

Wedding Rings Online
Make it a habit to check for products through *Yahoo.com* or other search engines. Why? Because you never know what treasure you may find. By entering thxe words "Wedding Rings" into a search engine, you might find directory of companies selling rings, as well as handcrafted and custom-designed rings made from everything such as solid billet titanium to Scottish gold—even priceless antique rings.

ServiceMerchandise.com is the online version of the nationwide store that offers a wide array of rings and diamonds.

http://www.servicemerchandise.com

Calculator.com is a useful site for several reasons. First, it "crawls" through the Web looking for the best prices on particular products or services. For example, by typing the word "wedding" into its search field, Calculator.com will reveal a list of several gold wedding and diamond wedding bands—complete with prices and links to those store where the rings are being sold! This site searches in several categories, including, hardware, software, entertainment, books, music, and more.

http://www.calculator.com

Registries Online
Surf the Web and you'll discover that it's the ideal medium for bridal registries. It's simple to register and select items. It's just as easy and convenient for guests to look up your name and find the items you've listed. Buying with a credit card is secure, and it takes only minutes to complete the purchase.

All-Purpose Wedding Registries

You'll find that all-purpose wedding sites—including those mentioned in the first chapter—offer extensive registries to go along with personalized wedding pages and announcements. But these are not the only registries online. Many manufacturers and department stores offer registries as well—so many, in fact, that the real problem becomes how to choose the ones you want!

WeddingNetwork.com—which is listed as one of the largest online gift registries, with over 35,000 products—is the "official on-line wedding registry" of *Modern Bride Magazine*.

http://www.weddingnetwork.com

In addition to the all-purpose wedding Web sites mentioned earlier, here are more that offer extensive registries:

http://www.shewey.com/wedding/indeximg.htm
http://www.usabride.com
http://www.4.theknot.com/registry.html
http://www.thegift.com

There's also YWH.com, which is not really a wedding site, but a dedicated Internet online registry featuring high quality products. This registry can be accessed at:

http://www.ywh.com/wedding/wedding.html

Department Store & Specialty Registries

The Web is populated by the finest department stores, specialty stores, even international bridal registries like Christofle—an internationally known store which has been specializing in the "arts de la table" since the age of Napoleon!

http://www.christofle.com/che11.htm

Most major retailers have "store locators" so you can find stores in your area. Here are some major retail registry sites:

http://www.bloomingdales.com
http://www.dillards.com
http://www.jcpenney.com/jcp/GiftRegistry
http://www.macysbridal.com
http://www.sears.com/prod/giftreg/wedding.htm
http://www.servicemerchandise.com
http://www.sharperimage.com
http://www.strouds.com

In Summary

With so many options and alternatives for gowns and registries, it's likely your head is swimming by now. If you are using the Web, don't be overwhelmed by all the sites. Find one or two that you feel comfortable with, and go more deeply into those. Always be guided by your personal dreams of what your gown should be like, as well as the wedding theme, style, and budget—and you won't go wrong. By narrowing your gown search you are one step closer to making dreams become reality. So keep looking, and remember that there are many ways to own and rent gowns.

The next wedding planning phase will stimulate the taste buds. In fact, it's all about the *sweet taste of good times* –which means cakes, catering, and good friends.

Chapter 4

Day 4— The Sweet Taste of Good Times

For some, the reception really begins the moment the bar opens, and when luscious plates of fresh fruit and hors d'oeuvres stream out of the kitchen. This planning chapter focuses on the theme of spicing up your special day with the sweet taste of food *and* good times.

Catering Planning

There are some "musts" or rules of thumb that will help ensure that you find the caterer that is best for you—and for your budget. Above all else, taste the food. Referrals and recommendations from others are good, but you still need to taste the food for yourself. Many caterers will make food tasting appointments. Both the bride and groom-to-be, as well as others involved in the planning need to be taste testers.

Make it a point to ask about the chef's experience, about the number of years the caterer has been in business, and about licensing. All caterers need to be licensed. Some states, in fact, require that caterers work out of kitchens that are licensed by the Health Department. Make sure a contract includes such things as clean-up, cake-cutting fees, corking fees, gratuities, rentals, and the guaranteed number of servers who will be present.

Catering is one of a wedding's most expensive items. It's

one of the most important, too. Some caterers have a minimum price, regardless of the number of guests—so ask and save yourself time if that caterer doesn't meet your budgetary requirements. The catering budget depends on the number of guests, and most caterers will usually add enough extra dinner portions to cover from 5 to 10% above the final number you confirm. But to be on the safe side, ask how many dinners will you be covered for in case extra guests show up—and get this number, or percentage in writing.

It's always nice if you can feed your photographer, musicians, and others who are working for you—so find out if the caterer can provide this group of people with sandwiches, salads, or other less costly food. Lastly, always request a written quote covering all charges so you can compare costs.

QUICK NOTES:

- Find caterers through personal referrals
- Always taste the food that you choose for your guests—both the bride and groom should be involved in the catering decision-making
- Find out if the caterer is licensed
- Inquire about caterer's experience and ask for referrals
- Ask if contract includes clean-up, cake-cutting fees, corking fees, gratuities
- Find out what rentals, if any, are included
- Get a guaranteed number of servers and staff
- Have the caterer agree to include extra dinner portions
- Always get a written estimate of charges

CATERING CHECKLIST

FEES & POLICIES
- Amount of Deposit/Date Required
- Postponement/Cancellation Policy
- Final Payment Due Date
- Security Deposit Needed
- Rental Fees (silver, linens, chairs, etc)
- Cake Cutting Fee
- Overtime Fees
- Contract
- Licensed Caterer & Licensed Kitchen
- Taxes & Gratuities Added
- Corking Fees
- Clean Up/Security Deposit
- References/Referrals
- Guaranteed Extra Guest Meal Percentage
- Minimum Catering Amount
- Name of Contact Person for other Vendors
- Liability Insurance

MENU & SERVICES
- Schedule Taste Test
- Menu Options (hors d'oeuvres, appetizers, entrees, salads, etc.)
- Cost Per Person
- Children's Menu/Pricing
- Garnishments for Buffet Table: Yes/No
- Meals for Photographers, Musicians, etc.

- Provide Seating Arrangement
- Coffee Service: Yes/No
- Non-alcoholic Beverages/Cost
- Alcoholic Beverages[Costs
- Kitchen Facilities
- Full Service Bar Facilities: Yes/No
- Bartender Provided: Yes/No
- # of Servers/Outfits They Will Wear
- Table Decoration/Centerpieces Provided: Yes/No
- Table Numbers Provided: Yes/No
- Extra Charges (For placement of favors, place cards, etc.)
- May Family Take Left Over Food
- Chairs, Linens, Tableware, Centerpieces

Smart Beverage Budget Tips

The combined budget for catering and beverages normally accounts for the lion's share of wedding expenses—commonly from 30 to 50% of the total bill. Typically, beverages can dramatically drive up the cost of catering—especially if alcoholic beverages are part of the equation.

Even if you include alcohol, there are ways, to limit consumption and cost. For example, you may decide to feature wine or champagne only—with a limit of one or two bottles for each table (that's about four to five full glasses per each bottle). Since people tend to consume less alcohol earlier in the day, an afternoon wedding will generally limit alcohol consumption—and cost. Reducing the time between the ceremony and the beginning of the reception will also cut down on drinking. Some weddings skip the open bar altogether—moving right from the ceremony to the lunch or the dinner.

Another idea that's gaining in popularity is that of having a non-alcoholic affair that features a juice and water bar, in addition to non-alcoholic wines, sparkling ciders, and champagnes. Others may opt for an international coffee bar that features cappuccino, espresso, and flavored coffee drinks.

If beverage cost is an issue, ask your caterer if he or she has any other economical suggestions or alternatives. You may be able to bring your own bottles of wine or beverages to the reception, although some caterers may charge an increased corking fee if the bottles are not their own.

QUICK NOTES:

- Reduce beverage cost by limiting alcoholic consumption
- Offer 1-2 bottles of wine or champagne per table
- Replace alcohol with non-alcoholic wines, sparkling ciders, and champagne
- Feature an international coffee bar with espresso and flavored drinks
- Include a complete juice and water bar
- Have an afternoon wedding, which cuts down on consumption
- Limit the open bar time, or skip the open bar by going directly from the ceremony to lunch or dinner
- Ask your caterer if you can bring your own bottles

Smart Catering Budget Tips

There was a time when wedding catering fell into two convenient categories: Sit down dinners and buffets. Today, however, wedding receptions can offer a wide variety of catering options, including brunches, hors d'oeuvres, high teas, and even dessert receptions. Each approach requires a different amount of labor. The result?—the lower the overhead, the less the overall catering cost.

Sit down dinners are classy and elegant, but they require more servers—usually one for every 8 to 10 guests. In comparison, the most lavish buffet or brunch weddings require only one server for every 20 to 25 guests. Always ask how many servers will be needed for the reception, and find out if this cost is figured into the overhead. Most often, it is. Sometimes, a minimum tip or gratuity is automatically figured into the bill.

Are off-site caterers more economical? Generally, they may be, except that there are additional charges that may not be required from a banquet hall. These could include things like the linen, place settings, silver, and other rental items. Only by getting a written estimate can you really compare your catering options.

QUICK NOTES:

- Lower overhead and labor to reduce catering costs
- Sit down dinners require one server for every 8-10 guests
- Buffet dinners require one server for every 20-25 guests
- Ask about gratuities, corking fees, and other hidden costs
- Find out additional costs of rental items from off-site caterers

Here are three ideas that might help trim the catering budget down to size. And, they may make planning for catering a little less stressful. The first option? Consider having a favorite restaurant host your wedding. At our own wedding, for example, we held the reception at a nearby restaurant—a romantic and intimate Italian restaurant in our community capable of holding up to 150 guests. Not only did they have an impressive, full service bar, but they worked with us to rearrange the tables and partition the room to create a separate space for the musicians. They let us use a large room for hors d'oeuvres, and arranged for a sign-in table and a large table for gifts. Unlimited soft drinks and coffee service were included with the sit down dinner—and there was no extra cake-cutting charge. Plus, a large parking lot adjoined the restaurant, so there was no need for valet parking or other charges. Except for a corking fee and gratuity charge, all these extras were included in a reasonable per person catering fee—and there was no rental charge for the space. Best of all, the food was piping hot, delicious, plentiful, and prepared with loving care and attention.

Depending on the size of your reception—and the size of the restaurant—you may have the entire restaurant to yourself. However, if the restaurant needs to "reopen" after your party, then you may not have the option of letting the wedding run "over."

A second option that can reduce the catering budget is the dessert reception. This may be ideal for those getting married for a second time who don't want a complete sit down dinner. The idea behind the dessert reception—popular in many high end hotels—is this: After an evening ceremony, as many guests as you want are invited to an extravagant dessert reception. Of course, you would have to indicate on the invitation that a "dessert reception" follows the ceremony.

The third option for lowering the budget cost is the English high tea. This European custom dates back to England and the early 19th century. It's perfect for late morning or early afternoon weddings, and creates a feeling of old world elegance that makes it a match for Victorian-themed weddings. High teas combine what are known as *savories* and *sweets*.

The savories consist of tasty sandwiches, salads, and appetizers. The sweets consist of fruit with pound cake, custard puffs, and sweet scones adorned with a delectable choice of jams and cream. In addition to tea and coffee, the traditional sherry is also served. While high teas are not labor intensive, they may require rental of silver and china. As with all catering options, write down all charges that are included.

QUICK NOTES:

- Use your favorite restaurant to save on rental fees and other banquet hall charges
- Find out how long the restaurant will stay "closed" for your reception

- Dessert receptions are ideal for second marriages or a large guest count
- English high teas offer buffet type savings with style

Cake Planning

This is one of the more anticipated parts of wedding planning. Referrals may be invaluable in locating the right cake. So ask your caterer, friends, and those who have gotten married recently. If you're lucky, you might have tasted the perfect cake at a wedding.

Make plans to visit the bakery in advance, just to look at their cake designs. Choose several cakes to taste—and have the bakery include their most popular or specialty cake. It always helps if you know the flavors you want to taste in advance.

Always ask about your cake's delivery, how long the frosting will last (your caterer may not be able to refrigerate the cake), and who will set up the cake's tiers and cake topper.

QUICK NOTES:

- Ask for baker referrals and recommendations from your caterer and friends
- Taste several flavors, including the bakery's specialty

Smart Cake Budget Tips

There are some ways to cut cake costs that are ingenious. For example, the top tiers of the cake can be real, while the remaining cake tiers are actually false bottoms. The rest of the cake is baked in large cake sheets and served from the kitchen.

Also, don't overlook grocery store bakers. They often bake wedding cakes—at a fraction of the cost. Again, always taste the goods before ordering.

QUICK NOTES:

- Cut cake costs with a false cake bottoms—and serve from cake sheets in the kitchen
- Ask local grocery store bakers if they bake wedding cakes

CAKE CHECKLIST

FEES & POLICIES
- Amount of Deposit/Date Required
- Postponement/Cancellation Policy
- Final Payment Due Date
- Cake Delivery Fee
- Contract
- Cake Guarantee/Back-up
- Cake Tier Set-up Fee: Yes/No
- Flower/Cake Topper Set-up Fee: Yes/No
- References/Referrals
- Name of Contact Person for other Vendors

SERVICES
- Schedule Taste Test
- Cake Fillings/Frostings
- Cost Per Person
- # of Cake Tiers
- Cake Delivery Time
- Refrigerated Delivery: Yes/No
- Length of Time Frosting Will Last

DAY 4—WEB TIPS & RESOURCE GUIDE

Catering Online

Since your caterer will be local, one of the best ways to find local vendors on the Web is with an Internet *Yellow Pages*, such as the ones powered by *Yahoo.com* and *Excite.com*. A third search engine, *Lycos.com*, uses the *GTE's Superpages*. For your reference, these three are included below.

After entering your address or region, try entering the words "caterers," "cakes," and "weddings" to pull up neighborhood vendors. For example, when we searched under the word "caterers," we found a list of 16 caterers in our immediate area!

http://yp.yahoo.com/

A second useful Internet Yellow Pages can be located at the folowing URL address:

http://yellowpages.zip2.com/

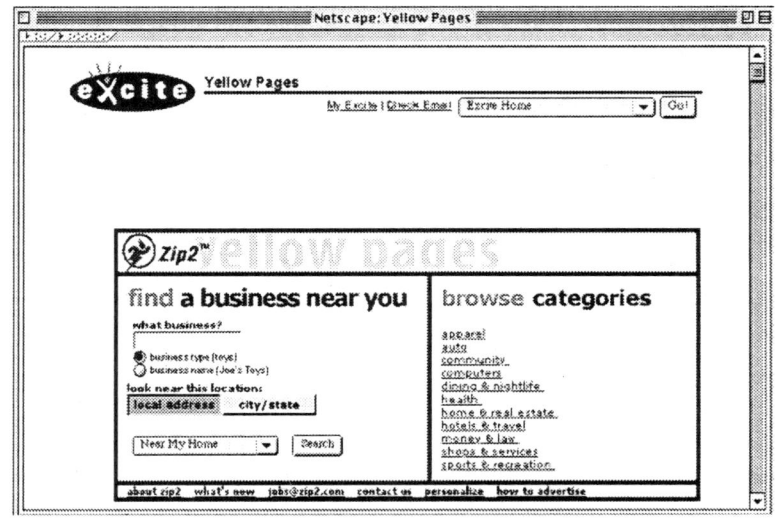

Here is the URL address for GTE's Superpages, a third useful Internet Yellow Pages resource:

http://yp.superpages.com/

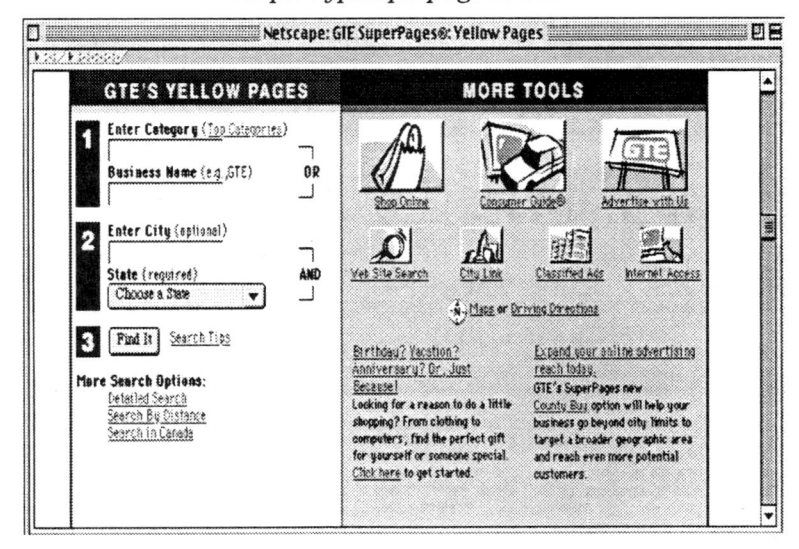

In Summary
Take your time when choosing the wedding menu and cake. Guests will appreciate the care you have taken. Besides, you may not get much of an opportunity to eat at your own wedding, so enjoy all the flavors that this phase of planning has to offer. By now, your wedding plans are really beginning to take shape. The upcoming wedding phase is just as exciting, challenging, and creative. It's the opportunity for you to begin *setting the perfect mood* in many ways.

Chapter 5

Day 5— Setting the Perfect Mood

There are several ways to set the mood for your wedding. Yet perhaps the most effective and powerful means are through the invitations, ceremony, and music. In this planning phase, you'll use the emotional appeal of these elements to craft a wedding that expresses your most heartfelt feelings and dreams.

Crafting the Ceremony

The setting, the music, the procession, the vows, the exchange of rings, and the kiss. Here is a true-to-life stage performance more compelling than anything accomplished by our greatest actors and actresses. Plus, there is the spontaneity that can only come from a live, emotionally charged moment as special as this. For these reasons, try to work out in advance as many details of your ceremony as possible. In this way you will ensure that the mood and feelings you want to express come through loud and clear.

Words are powerful. They can elevate our spirits and even move us to tears. The words you—as the bride and groom—choose to add to the ceremony can be a powerful statement of your love and commitment. If the officiator is willing to let you include favorite readings, get a copy of the officiator's standard written ceremony, so you can look for places to add your special words. Where do you find this material? Try looking at your most loved spiritual or religious texts, or poetry. In particular, look for readings that connect to the themes of love and marriage that express your deepest, innermost feelings. These could cover ideas like empathy, compassion, sharing, and respect. Then, think about having someone special—either parents or those in the wedding party—read from these selections. This is an honor, and it adds some variety to the ceremony.

Because there are many religious wedding customs and traditions, modern ceremonies vary greatly—such as the order for walking down the aisle, the music, participation of parents and others may vary from wedding to wedding. For traditional wedding etiquette guidance, consider books such as those by Emily Post, or ask your clergy.

It is important to have one or two people who can supervise the ceremony and ensure that everything runs smoothly. This trusted individual needs to make sure that all miscellaneous items and decorations are in place, such as candles, ring pillow, flowers, ribbons—even birdseed for the guests to shower the newly-weds after the ceremony.

This supervisor should also prepare the bride, groom, and others for any last minute details before the ceremony begins—like making sure everyone has the right bouquet, corsage, or boutonniere. And, he or she needs to coordinate the timing and placement of musicians, photographers, and others.

If possible, try to get everything in place the night before, or the morning of the ceremony. Musicians, if you have them, should be seated or in position and playing walk-in music anywhere up to a half-hour before the ceremony is scheduled to begin.

A beautifully designed wedding program—placed on chairs or handed out by a wedding party usher at the door—adds a touch of charm and lets guests know what to expect. It also serves as a keepsake and can even include a prayer or blessing that is incorporated into the ceremony. The program can include the names of the bride and groom, the wedding party, the date, and a listing of each wedding element as it is to occur—seating of family, musical selection, processional, candle lighting, readings, and vows, etc. You can create programs on your computer, if you have one, or get program printing included with your invitation estimate.

If there's time—and if the budget permits—have the photographer take pictures of people arriving, including candid shots of the bride and others before the ceremony begins.

QUICK NOTES:

- Look to favorite spiritual, religious, or poetry to add special readings
- Have wedding party or other special persons read selections
- Appoint one or two persons to supervise the ceremony
- Set-up the ceremony site and miscellaneous items as much in advance as allowed
- Play music 30 minutes before during seating and before ceremony
- Hand out printed wedding programs with names of bride, groom, wedding party, and chronology of events
- Have photographer take candid, pre-ceremony shots

CEREMONY CHECKLIST

- Confirm set-up time
- Confirm with musicians/photographer/officiator
- Confirm seating Arrangement
- Obtain copy of ceremony
- Choose pre-ceremony, walk-in music
- Choose processional music
- Coordinate ceremony music with officiator
- Secure separate bride's room
- Prepare candles and other items

- Give rings to appropriate persons
- Hand out bouquets, corsages, and boutonnieres
- Coordinate photographer and musicians
- Have Ushers and others in place
- Get procession line in order
- Begin procession with music
- Establish receiving line order
- Distribute birdseed or confetti for guests
- Clean up, collect keepsake items, and bring Unity Candle and flowers to reception as needed

Music Planning

Planning the music for a wedding ceremony and reception can seem daunting—especially if you're not musically inclined. But don't worry. There are many excellent wedding musicians, wedding music CDs, and a long history of wedding music for every taste and style. The most important thing you'll need to decide is what kind of music fits into your budget. There is a wide range of live music that can bring your ceremony to life—from the traditional organ or harp, to a four piece ensemble complete with a vocalist. If your budget only calls for recorded CDs or cassettes, there are a host of wedding collections from which to choose.

If you should opt for live music, how do you pick the right musician? For this, you might want to look around for referrals. Ask your caterer and other vendors for recommendations. Musicians should provide you with selection assistance, and above all, be professional. Before meeting any musician, and to save time, always ask for a demo cassette tape.

Listening to demo tapes will also give you ideas about what music you like. You may, for example, love the sound or particular instrument. However, only by listening to the actual instruments will you know if it's right for your wedding. Some musicians specialize in certain kinds of music—such as classical—while you may want some modern love songs and themes played during the ceremony walk-in period. Music sets the tone for your ceremony—so be sure the musician or musicians can deliver exactly you want.

Once you find a musician you like, make sure that the contract stipulates that he or she is the one who will be present and playing at your ceremony. Lastly, remember to ask about overtime charges. Many ceremonies start later than planned, and you want to be sure your musicians will be present in case things run over.

Reception music runs the gamut from string ensembles during cocktail hour, to a full orchestra, band, or a DJ to set the mood and generate fun. If you get a chance, go see the band or DJ play live at another wedding. This will give you a real solid feeling for how they perform and work with the guests. A live band tends to take a bigger bite out of the budget than a DJ with a light show. If there's special music you'd like—such as an ethnic selection—tell the band or DJ far in advance. The DJ will normally obtain this music at his/her expense.

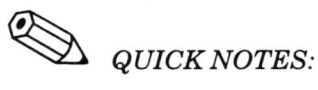

QUICK NOTES:

- Fit music to your budget
- Ask for demo video or demo cassette tape before meeting with musicians
- Make sure musicians can play the style and selections you want
- Stipulate in the contract that there are no substitutions for the DJ,. Band, or musicians you want
- Know the overtime fee, and require that they be available in case the wedding lasts longer
- DJ's will obtain special requests, such as ethnic songs, at their expense

MUSIC CHECKLIST

FEES & POLICIES
- Amount of Deposit/Date Required
- Postponement/Cancellation Policy
- Final Payment Due Date
- Contract
- Guarantee Named Performers/DJ
- Number of instruments
- Minimum fee
- Hourly Rate
- Overtime Rate
- Number & length of breaks
- Confirm time of arrival/Set-up
- References/Referrals
- Name of Contact Person for other Vendors
- Liability Insurance

SERVICES
- Requested Songs
- DJ provides requested selections: Yes/No
- Choose first dance selection
- Emcee: Yes/No
- Musician/DJ attire
- Band/DJ play list
- Karaoke: Yes/No
- Lighting Effects: Yes/No

Invitation Planning

The wedding invitation is the first tangible thing guests have to hold in their hands and to look at. No wonder it set the tone for all that follows. Whether an invitation is uncommonly distinctive, whimsical, or an expression of simple elegance, it helps guests anticipate the wedding day event.

After choosing the invitation and completing the wording, printing is relatively fast. As far as the envelopes, these are usually handwritten or addressed in calligraphy style.

One easy and quick way to determine an invitation's wording is to look at samples. Many invitation printers will oblige. Some will even assist in the wording process. If a reception immediately follows the ceremony, this may also be noted on the invitation. Receptions in other locations may be printed on a separate card—with a map on the card or included separately. You'll also have to include RSVP cards and a self-addressed, stamped reply envelope.

A word about postage. Most invitations with reply cards require two stamps. Even if it weighs just an ounce, the oversize envelope may *still* require that second stamp—so don't take any chances. Take the completed invitation to the post office to figure the correct postage amount.

QUICK NOTES:

- Invitations set the tone
- Use sample invitations to find your ideal wording
- Use calligraphy or handwriting for addressing invitations
- Be safe by using two stamps on your invitation

Smart Invitation Budget Tips

Some invitations use engraved printing, which is more expensive and raises the lettering slightly. However, a process known as thermographic printing can reduce the budget by as much as 50%, and still produce high quality printing in most color inks.

INVITATION CHECKLIST

FEES & POLICIES
- Amount of Deposit/Date Required
- Postponement/Cancellation Policy
- Final Payment Due Date
- Printing Date Due
- Contract
- Total Fee
- References/Referrals
- Name of Contact Person for other Vendors

SERVICES
- Ink Color
- Printing Type (engraved/thermographic)
- Font/Letter Style
- Check Final Proof Sheet before printing
- Total # of invitations/return cards
- Maps
- # Extra envelopes
- Lining included: Yes/No
- Order "Thank You" cards
- Wedding Program printing: Yes/No
- Additional items (such as printing for napkins and favors)

DAY 5—WEB TIPS & RESOURCE GUIDE

Music Online

To find music for your ceremony and reception, you can use all three methods we've introduced thus far:

1) Use an Internet Yellow Pages search under the words "music," "wedding music," and "DJs"
2) Search via any of the all-purpose wedding sites
3) Search for specialty music Web sites.

Because practice makes perfect, here's another look at the basic Internet Yellow Pages. Since these tend to come in handy, you can "bookmark," or save, these addresses within your Web browser:

http://yp.yahoo.com/
http://yellowpages.zip2.com/
http://yp.superpages.com/

UltimateWedding.com is one all-purpose wedding site providing unique music offerings. Its Ultimate Wedding Song Library organizes music by section—including reception music, ceremony music, and a DJ search by geographic location. Within each section you will find categories, such as Couple's First Dance, that show the most requested dance songs taken from an online survey.

In addition, this Web site contains sound clips for about 400 clips of songs are offered online! (Keep in mind that you may need to download the RealAudio Player to hear the sound clips.)

You can find the Ultimate Wedding Song Library at:

http://www.weddingromance.com/songs

(see picture next page)

Netscape: Ultimate Wedding Song Library (including Sound Clips) with over 400 songs
Ultimate Wedding Song Library
Hundreds of songs to help you choose the perfect music for your special day!
Congratulations, you're ENGAGED!!!
You've been dreaming about your wedding day for years, the gown, the flowers, the music ... MUSIC!
We have all the resources you need to choose the perfect music for your special day!!
Sign up for our monthly wedding planning & resource newsletter
Enter your email address and press
Submit
Wedding Song Survey - Please take a moment to add the songs you will be having at your ceremony and reception!
If you are a wedding professional, click here
Reception Music
Ceremony Music
COUPLE'S FIRST DANCE
PRELUDE

Musicblvd.com is a Web store where you can search for "wedding" and bring up more than 31 different wedding CDs—including country, classical, and even Irish wedding collections.

http://www.musicblvd.com

Two more all-purpose sites, WedNet.com and Wedding-world.com, provide geographic locators for finding musicians.

http://www.wednet.com/vendors/regionindex.asp
http://wedding-world.com/musicians.html

ProDJ.com is a specialty Internet search engine for finding DJs and DJ companies throughout the US, Canada, and around the world. There are thousands of mobile DJs listed, even in small towns and regional areas. This very comprehensive Web site is located at:

http://www.prodj.com/ep/index.html

(see picture next page)

Cmusic.com, known as Complete Music, is a nationwide DJ company. Their DJ Locator lets you click on a map to find DJs in your local area.

http://www.cmusic.com/map.html

Invitations Online

Almost anything you can think of in the way of invitations is available on the Web. You can either visit an all-purpose site to find the perfect invitation, or you can try some of these suggestions.

Invitationshoppe.com offers over 500 different kinds of handmade papers.

http://invitationshoppe.com/

Invitations4you.com features over 4500 invitations to choose from. They say they can finish printing an order in five days or less. Plus, they ship anywhere in the U.S.

http://www.invitations4you.com

Since there are many invitation resources on the Internet, here are some additional ones that may be worth checking out:

http://wedding-world.com/invitations.html
http://www.invitationsplus.com/
http://www.greetingsfrom.invitations.com/
http://www.discount-invitations.com/

Maps Online

How would you like to have an instant map showing your ceremony and reception sites? It's possible online, thanks to sites such as MapBlast.com and MapQuest.com. These sites help take the drudgery out of drawing a map of your wedding sites by actually printing out a detailed map within seconds!

Simply enter in the address of your reception, home or other site, and get a neighborhood map that is easy to print from any computer. Then, photocopy the map and presto—instant invitation maps.

http://www.mapquest.com
http://www.mapblast.com

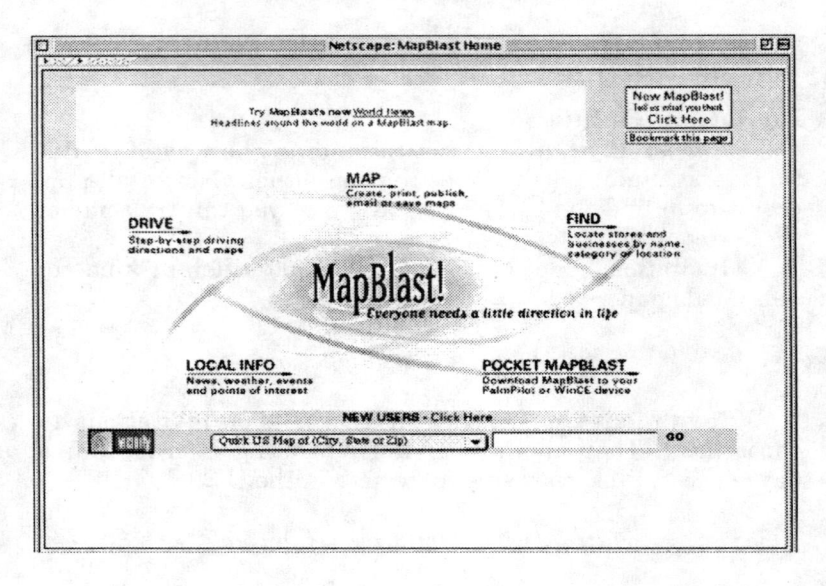

In Summary

Creating the perfect mood is a fun, satisfying experience worth the effort. Even after you've found the ideal ensemble, band, orchestra, or DJ, take your time in listening to the songs you want during the ceremony and reception. The time you spend now will pay dividends on your big day. The next chapter, with the theme of *looking good*, will give you long-lasting enjoyment as well. After all, while the wedding lasts for only a single day, the photographs last for a lifetime.

Chapter 6

Day 6— Looking Very, Very Good

Good photographers and videographers deliver the kind of memories that last forever. That's why it's worth finding talented professionals to do the job. Good photographers can be found at bridal shows, through referrals, and even over the Internet. So, while you may have a friend or uncle who offers photographic services, unless they're proven photographers, the results may not measure up.

Photography Planning

Always look at a photographer's portfolio so you can examine the quality and style of their work. Speaking of styles, they change over time. So, too, have styles of wedding photography. One recent popular style is that of *black and white* photography. Shot on black and white film, these photographs have a classic, dramatic look that is beautiful and quite stunning. If this style appeals to you, but don't want the entire wedding shot this way, you can compromise and opt to have only black and white portraits of the bride and groom—taken either before or after the ceremony.

Another style that is popular? *Photojournalism*. This gets its name because the shots are candid, not posed. Photographers often use long lenses so they can take pictures unobtrusively from across the room. Not every photographer is experienced at this style, so be sure to examine at the photographer's work. Then again, you can always place disposable cameras on each table for guests to snap away all the candid shots they want.

Whatever style a photographer uses, he or she should tell the whole story of your wedding, including: The arrival of the bride and wedding party at the ceremony, the first dance, the guests, a close-up showing the rings as the bride and groom hold hands, the bouquet and the garter toss, the gift table, the bride and groom as they are chauffeured away, and more.

Good photographers get booked up far in advance, especially on Saturday nights—so once you find one you like, go ahead and make the booking. And get it in writing the name of the person who will take your photographs.

Smart Photography Budget Tips

Once you're satisfied with a photographer's portfolio, you'll need to compare prices and budgets. Often, this can be confusing. There may be prices for individual portraits, family portraits, the cost of albums, and additional prints. It will be easier if you can figure out in advance what you want in the way of prints. Then, try to get estimates based on those needs. Do you want the photographer take photographs at the rehearsal dinner, as well as at bridal showers and bachelor parties? If so, be sure to have him or her include this in the estimate.

A simpler way is to pay for the photographer's time. Ask the photographer to give you his or her *a la carte* or *artistry only* rates. Basically, this equates into an hourly rate with a minimum number of hours, plus materials—so you pay only for what you need. How can this save you money? If, for example, you receive a photo album as a gift, then you won't need one included with your photographer's package.

QUICK NOTES:

- *Black and white* photography and portraits can add a dramatic twist to a wedding album
- *Photojournalism* style makes for striking candid photography
- Photographer needs to tell the story of the wedding from beginning to end
- Decide if you want to include rehearsal dinner, showers, and bachelor party pictures
- Figure out how many prints you want
- Ask photographers for *artistry only* or *a la carte* rates to save

PHOTOGRAPHY CHECKLIST

FEES & POLICIES
- Amount of Deposit/Date Required
- Postponement/Cancellation Policy
- Final Payment Due Date
- Contract
- Package Rate
- Artistry Only Rate
- A La Carte Rate
- Cost for Overtime
- Cost to buy negatives
- Date to Review Proofs
- References/Referrals

- Name of Contact Person for other Vendors
- Liability Insurance

SERVICES
- # of Prints
- Sizes of Prints
- Album(s) Included: Yes/No
- Engagement/Bridal Portraits
- Photojournalism Style: Yes/No
- Black & White Style: Yes/No
- Review Final Proofs before printing

Videography Planning

Not so many years ago, wedding videography was a costly extravagance. Over time, however, it became affordable and is now considered essential by many. Videography doesn't replace photographs, but it certainly adds to them. Just to have the entire ceremony videotaped for posterity makes the cost worthwhile.

As with photography, hiring a professional wedding videographer is worth the investment. Here are a few helpful hints for judging a videographer's work. Are the shots well lit? Are they in focus? Can you clearly hear the sound? Do the scenes cut together seamlessly? Does the video include graphics and background music for a polished, professional look?

Videography presents some issues that can affect the finished product, as well as the budget. The most basic videography shoot uses just one camera. Two and three camera video shoots provide greater coverage of the event and allow for intercutting within the same scene. For example, a wide shot of the bride walking down the aisle can cut to a close-up on the groom's face as he watches her approach. Each additional camera requires another camera operator, which increases the budget. Editing the final wedding video takes a lot longer, too, when there are more shots to look at.

At the reception, the videographer should pause long enough to allow guests at each table to give their best wishes to the bride and groom. Like the photographer, the videographer tells the complete story of the wedding.

Smart Videography Budget Tips

Should you hire one videographer to shoot the wedding, you can *still* get a two-camera set up for almost no additional cost. Here's how. Simply put an extra video camera into service during the ceremony and the reception. If you don't have one, find a friend or family member who is willing to lend a camera. Place this second camera on a tripod at the back of the ceremony hall. Zoom out the lens to provide a wide angle shot, and begin recording when the ceremony starts. Give the videotape to the videographer, who can easily edit these wide angle shots into the video. The same camera can be set up to take pictures of the head table during the reception. This is simple and easy, since no-one has to attend to the camera once it is focused on the bride and groom and the record button is pushed. Coordinate this effort with the videographer to get specifics, such as recording speed, lighting, and other technical considerations.

The videographer should provide you with a finished, edited version of the wedding—and give you the unedited "raw" videotapes. Finally, know in advance what kind of graphics or music will be edited in the final videotape, and get this in writing.

QUICK NOTES:

- Look for the smoothness, lighting, and sound quality in video samples
- If your budget calls for a one camera shoot, look at one camera videotapes
- Have a spare camera set-up for a wide angle shot at the ceremony for an extra camera from which to edit

- The Videographer should tell the entire wedding story, with comments from individuals
- Make sure contract provides for a final edited version, the kind of graphics and music to be included, and the unedited videotapes

VIDEOGRAPHY CHECKLIST

FEES & POLICIES
- Amount of Deposit/Date Required
- Postponement/Cancellation Policy
- Final Payment Due Date
- Contract
- Package Rate (Editing/Shooting/Graphics)
- Cost for Overtime
- Date to Review Video
- References/Referrals
- Name of Contact Person for other Vendors
- Liability Insurance

SERVICES
- # of finished Videos
- Printed Labels/Covers Yes/No
- Review First Cut for Approval
- Hand over raw, unedited footage

Out-of-town Accommodations

Major hotels make it easy to book rooms for weddings. One easy way is for the bride and groom-to-be to call the hotel and reserve the correct number of rooms under their name. Each room is given a confirmation number, which you can give to the guests. The guests call—usually a toll-free number—and give the confirmation number and pay by credit card. That's all there is to it.

You might want to ask your guests in advance if they have some special needs—a smoking or non-smoking room, a king-size bed, and so on. Some hotels have special rates for wedding parties—even if you're not having the wedding reception at that particular hotel—so make sure to ask.

Out-of-town guests have traveled a long way to be with you. As a token of appreciation, you could arrange for a "welcome basket"—containing fruit, bottled water or juice, a map, or anything else you think they would like—to be waiting for them when they arrive at the room. It's a special way of saying that you're glad they've come to share your special moment.

QUICK NOTES:

- Find out the number of rooms needed, and reserve these under your wedding party name
- Let guests know you've made reservations and give them confirmation numbers
- Find out special needs of out-of-town guests
- Prepare for a welcome basket to greet guests when they arrive at their room

DAY 6—WEB TIPS & RESOURCE GUIDE

Photography & Videography Online
Use the all purpose wedding sites or the Web *Yellow Pages* to find nearby wedding photographers and videographers. Just in case you didn't remember those Web addresses, here they are again:

http://yp.yahoo.com/
http://yellowpages.zip2.com/
http://yp.superpages.com/

Boecks.com is a company specializing in disposable wedding cameras. The unique thing about these 35mm cameras is that they come in several attractive designs, are beautifully boxed, and even contain instructions for the guests! All the cameras have a built-in flash and battery. Designs include the "rose garden," "tuxedo classic," and "Boecks Classic" look. For the most formal of occasions, they even offer a variety of classy, satin covered boxes.

http://www.boecks.com

Hotel Accommodations Online

Use the online Yellow Pages and type in the name of your desired hotel. Depending on the hotel, you may even be able to make reservations online.

Fodor's, the popular travel guide publisher, features a travel online hotel and restaurant index. This can be found at:

http://www.fodors.com

Another useful travel-related Web site is Trip.com. This site can be used to check prices on flights, and is especially helpful if you're picking up visiting guests from the airport. Trip.com features a "flight tracker" that lets you know whether flights are on time or delayed.

www.trip.com

In Summary

Once the photographers and videographers begin working at your wedding, you'll hardly notice them. But you'll long remember their efforts in making your wedding memorable. The next planning theme of *flowers & style fit for a bride and groom* will be remembered, too, as you beautify the entire wedding.

Chapter 7

Day 7— Flowers & the Perfect Fit

The addition of flowers and greenery at weddings is more than a tradition. Flower decorations make tables, altars, arches, and even cakes brighten with life and color. The presence of flowers and plants offer a lively affirmation of the blossoming of all wonderful things life provides, including love. This day's theme will give you some planning, creative, and budget tips for making a stylish statement using both flowers and wedding attire.

Flower Planning & Smart Budget Tips

There are several ways to obtain flowers, and even more ways to use them to set the mood and brighten the decorations. The first question you may be asking is: How do I choose the right florist?

Your budget may determine the quantity and type of flowers you can afford. Fortunately, there are ways to stretch your budget and get more flowers. In part, this depends on who you choose to do your flowers. The basic choices include a traditional cash and carry florist, a "home" florist or horticulturist, and friends who love gardening and are willing to provide arrangements as their wedding gift. If you opt for the professional florist, choose one that specializes in weddings and can provide photos of previous work.

A less costly option is to hire a horticulturist or flower arranger who works out of his or her home. For this, you can negotiate an hourly rate, plus materials and flowers. Arranging flowers is extremely labor intensive—so if you decide to do this yourself or work with others, make sure you are not shorthanded or lacking in experienced flower arrangers and expert bouquet-makers. To do any less would be to jeopardize your special day and add a level of stress that is best avoided the day before—and morning of—your wedding.

Then there's the matter of flowers. If you live near a wholesale flower mart, you might find some of the best deals on roses, tulips, and other typically expensive flowers. One good way to stretch the flower budget is to use seasonal flowers. These not only look good, but tend to be less expensive. Another idea? Silk flowers can be mixed in the with real thing to help fill out any arrangement. Silk bouquets, for example, can cost half as much as real flowers.

Here's another way to stretch the flower budget. Visit local nurseries—even a local garden club—to find plants, flowers, and ferns that are ideal for centerpieces. Of course, some restaurants and other reception sites include some kind of table decoration.

For home weddings, you might want to make dramatic changes to the backyard by adding the addition of very large plants. Fortunately, it's easy to rent these for the weekend from plant rental stores found in larger cities through the regular (or Web) Yellow Pages.

QUICK NOTES:

- Flowers services for all budgets come from sources like cash and carry flower shops, homegrown florists and horticulturists, and friends with love of gardening
- Ask to look at a vendor's previous wedding decorations

- Use both seasonal flowers and silk flowers to save more
- Consider plants as centerpieces
- Contact a local garden club or nursery
- Some restaurants and sites include table settings and centerpieces
- Rent larger plants for home weddings

Bridal Bouquet Preservation

Can the bridal bouquet be preserved? Yes—that is, if you have the right flowers, such as anemone, aster, baby's breath, bachelor button, button mum, carnation, camellia, dahlia, dogwood, larkspur, lilac, magnolia, marigold, pansy, poppy, rose, snap dragon, statice, and violet. Some flowers, however, are difficult to preserve. In general, steer away from iris and gardenias, succulent tropical flowers, and bulb flowers like orchids. Even after they have been dried, some flowers may alter color or crumble when exposed to humidity. Usually, flowers need to be dried, then sealed with a finisher to protect them.

Should you attempt to do this yourself, consider air drying or using silicon gel. Two books that describe how to perform this magic include *Flower Drying Art with Silicon Gel* and *The Best Flower Drying Book*. Also, there are companies that specialize in this service.

FLORIST CHECKLIST

FEES & POLICIES
- Amount of Deposit/Date Required
- Postponement/Cancellation Policy
- Final Payment Due Date
- Contract
- Time of Delivery/Set-up
- Ceremony Cost:

- Reception Cost:
- Bouquets/Corsages/Boutonnieres Cost:
- Centerpiece Cost:
- Head Table/Tables Cost:
- References/Referrals
- Name of Contact Person for other Vendors
- Liability Insurance

SERVICES
- # and type of Ceremony Decorations
- # and type of Reception Decorations
- Extra plants
- # of Centerpieces
- Bridal Bouquet
- # of Bridesmaids Bouquets
- # of Corsages
- # of Boutonnieres
- Flower Girl flowers/basket
- Review First Cut for Approval
- Hand over raw, unedited footage

Tuxedo Fitting

Since this chapter is about *style*, it includes the groom's tuxedo selection and fitting. Without a doubt, men have it considerably easier than women when it comes to wedding attire. A black tuxedo is the standard—except in warmer climates where a formal, white tuxedo is right at home.

Which tux looks the best—single or double-breasted? That is up to personal taste, although the single-breasted with a tail is considered the most formal and traditional.

After settling on a tuxedo style, it usually comes down to figuring out what kind of tie, cuff-links, vest, and shoes to wear. This is relatively painless, fast, and easily accomplished from several months to just weeks prior to the wedding. Accessories like the vest, tie, or cuff-links can be matched to the wedding color scheme, but this isn't usually necessary. Because you want to be absolutely sure the tux fits perfectly, always try it on before taking it home. Generally, tuxes can be picked up a day or two before the wedding, and returned the following week.

Smart Tuxedo Budget Tips

Keep in mind that some tuxedo companies offer a free tux for the groom—provided that several ushers and the best man also get their tuxes from the same shop. Always ask the proprietor about this policy.

QUICK NOTES:

- Always try on the fitted tux at the store before taking it home
- Ask about free tux policy for groom

TUXEDO CHECKLIST

FEES & POLICIES
- Amount of Deposit/Date Required
- Postponement/Cancellation Policy
- Final Payment Due Date
- Contract
- Fitting/Pick-up Date:
- Tux Return Date:
- Total Cost:

SERVICES
- Tux Style
- Accessories (tie, cuff links, buttons)
- Shoes
- Extras

Gown Fitting

If the gown has been sized right the first time, there should be no major surprises at this fitting. If there's a discrepancy, ask to be measured again. A proper sizing means there's no reason to pay for extra alterations. This is a good reason to ask for a copy of all the original measurements.

DAY 7—WEB TIPS & RESOURCE GUIDE

Flowers Online

By now, you're all too familiar with the Web Yellow Pages refrain. We'd repeat the addresses here, but you probably know them by heart! Instead, let's move on to some Web sites that may be of interest.

Wedding-world.com is an all-purpose wedding site with a florist's locator:

http://wedding-world.com/florists.html

FTD.com contains a convenient city/ state/ and zip code locator for finding an FTD florist. They are certainly ubiquitous, so you should be able to find one wherever you live. Also, consider this site as a source for out-of-town gift baskets, and for flower-girl and ring bearer gifts.

http://www.ftd.com

(see picture next page)

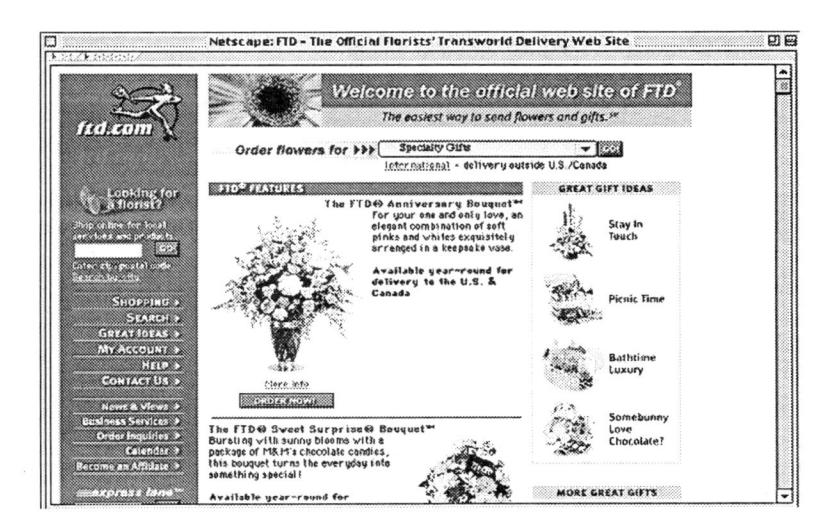

FleursPerMail.com offers a broad selection of silk bridal bouquets and arrangements for weddings.

http://www.fleurspermail.com

Bridal Bouquet Preservation Online

Forever Yours Keepsakes, Ltd. preserves those one-of-a-kind bridal and other floral arrangements.

http://www.westnet.com/fyk

Paula's Petals is a company that specializes in freeze drying flowers and bouquets. They create displays—that can include the invitation or other memento—in a variety of shadow boxes, and can even replace damaged flowers.

http://www.paulaptl.qpg.com

Blooming-color.com carefully presses each flower, then preserves bouquets in their original shape. They will even preserve the boutonniere inside what they call a "bridal flower picture."

http://blooming-color.com

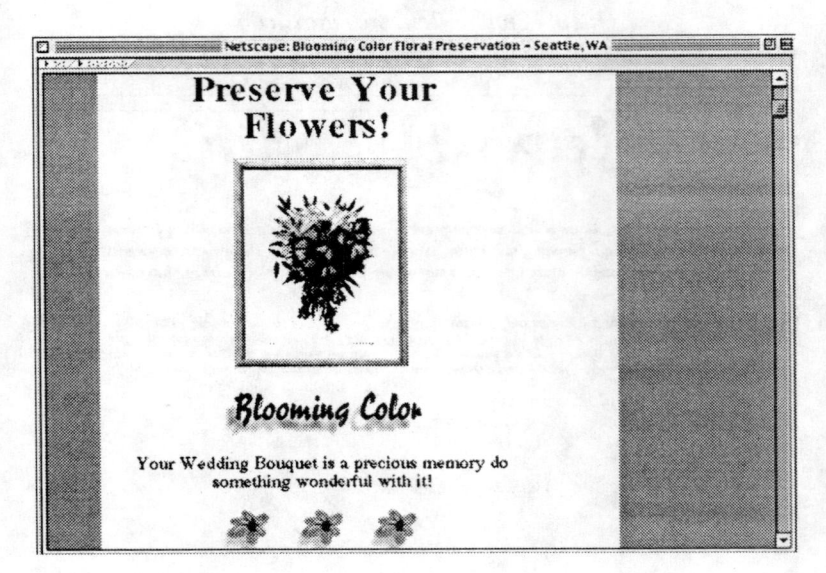

Tuxedos Online

Whether you shop for tuxes through the Web Yellow Pages, all-purpose wedding sites, or through Web Tux stores, you're likely to find what you're looking for. In addition to renting a tuxedo, it's also easy to purchase a tux—as illustrated by the sites below.

One place to find tuxedo stores is through the International Formalwear Association's Retail Store Locator. This locator allows you to search nationwide for association members.

http://www.formalwear.org/public/retailers/

There are many large tuxedo stores that service large regional areas, such as Ascottuxedos.com advertises over 70 stores in Texas and Louisiana.

http://www.ascottuxedos.com/home

1800MyTuxes.com is really Gino's Fashion Tuxedos, a NY store that ships tuxes just about anywhere.

http://www.1800MyTuxes.com

Tuxedos4u.com links to After Six, a tuxedo retailer that sells through a network of nationwide, authorized retailers.

http://www.tuxedos4u.com

Tuxonthenet.com is Smalls FormalWear—a regional chain of 70 rental stores covering an eight state area including New York, Pennsylvania, Maryland, Delaware, New Jersey, Virginia, Maine, and Connecticut. They offer things like a "measurement card" and a "Guide to Tuxedos and Formal Fashion."

http://www.tuxonthenet

Some Tuxedo stores on the Web rent and sell new, name brand tuxedos. While some stores may offer discounted prices, always shop and compare before buying. Here is a short list.

www.sirknight.com
http://www.tuxedonet.com
http://www.etuxedo.com

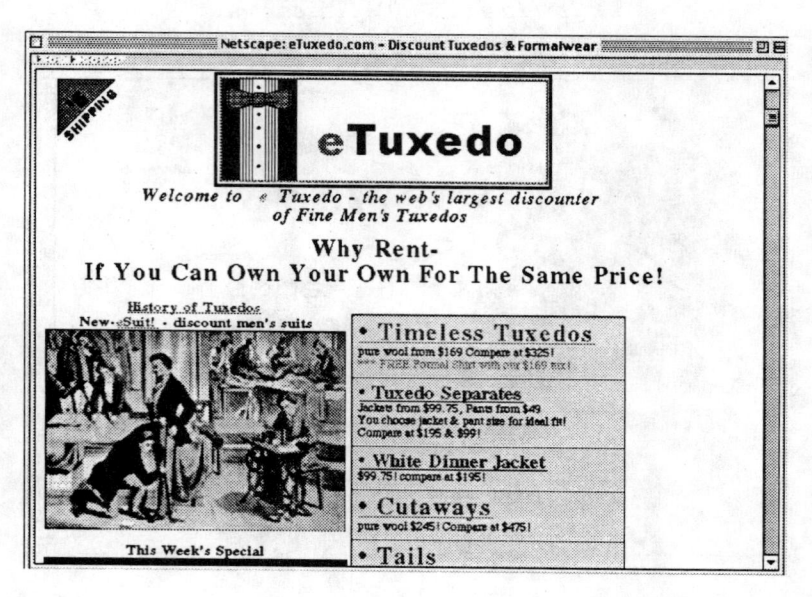

Lastly, here are two all-purpose wedding Web sites where you can search for tuxedos.

http://wedding-world.com/tuxedos.html
http://www.wednet.com/vendors/regionindex.asp

In Summary

With flower arrangements taken care of, you have solved most of the major wedding planning challenges. From this point forward, you'll be focusing on details and coordinating various wedding vendors. There's a lot of action ahead, and much of it involves things that have already been set in motion. No wonder that the next planning theme is a time of action, as you prepare to *rev up your chariot's engine*.

Chapter 8

Day 8— Rev Up Your Chariot's Engine

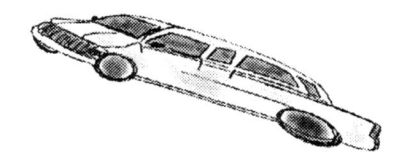

Welcome to a planning time when things really begin to take off—both literally, and figuratively. That's because you'll be planning your limousine transportation, as well as sending off invitations and obtaining your wedding license. First, let's look at what to expect when renting your own private chariot.

Limousine Planning

A ride in a long, stretch limo with champagne and all the amenities is a fairy-tale end to the wedding day. That's why, when it comes to the limo, it's important to plan in advance. True, you may be able to hire one at the last minute, but it may not be the color you requested, or it may be larger—and more costly—than you need. The moral of all this? Ideally, try to make arrangements at least two or three months before the wedding date—longer if you're getting married at the height of the wedding season or the prom season when limousines are in high demand.

Smart Limousine Budget Tips

Limousine companies usually have wedding package rates. Often, these include a basic fee for a minimum amount of time—

typically from three to four hours. Find out what's included in the package, such as champagne and other beverages, a *Just Married* sign, special music, flowers, and other decorations.

Always ask the year and make of the limousine. Why is this relevant? Not only do the styles change, but newer models are less likely to have mechanical problems—especially with the air conditioning during the summer months. Once you agree on the limousine to be used, make sure this is written in the contract.

QUICK NOTES:

- Book the limousine far in advance; earlier if at the height of the wedding season or during "prom" time
- Find what's included in wedding package
- Request a new limousine and get it in writing
- What decorations or signs are included

LIMOUSINE CHECKLIST

FEES & POLICIES
- Amount of Deposit/Date Required
- Postponement/Cancellation Policy
- Final Payment Due Date
- Contract
- Arrival Time/Location
- Drop Off Time/Location
- Minimum Time
- Wedding Package Cost
- Hourly Cost
- Mileage/Gas Fees
- References/Referrals

- Name of Contact Person for other Vendors
- Back-up Limo Guarantee
- Licensed/Insured

SERVICES
- Year/Make of Limousine
- Limousine Size/Capacity & Color
- Chauffeur's Attire
- Champagne Included: Yes/No
- Other Beverages: Yes/No
- Get Married Sign: Yes/No
- Flowers/Decorations: Yes/No
- Additional Amenities: TV/Music/Tapes
- Contingency Plan for Weather/Delays

Get the Wedding License

Every state has its own requirements for getting a wedding license. That's why we recommend first calling the government office—usually the City or County Clerk's office—that's in charge of this. In Los Angeles, for example, the Registrar-Recorder/Country Clerk's office handles marriage licenses. Usually, wedding licenses remain valid for a period of time, then expire. So make sure your wedding occurs within the proper, allowable time frame.

To apply for a wedding license, both the bride and groom-to-be must both be present. You may find that certain documents are needed, such as a driver's license, social security card, information documenting name changes—and don't forget that check or money order. Some states have a waiting period before issuing a license. In others, like California, you can obtain your wedding license that same day. The point is this—find out your state's regulations and what you need in advance, and you'll save a lot of time and trouble.

Once you've got the license, you are not legally married. It needs to be completed by your ceremony officiator—who will sign it and fill in some more information. Send in the signed and completed document, and your marriage is both legal and official. Getting the wedding license can be an exciting event. Make an outing of it, have a picnic or lunch or dinner to celebrate the joyous change in life you are about to take.

QUICK NOTES:

- Call your local City or County Clerk's office for requirements
- Gather all documents in advance, and go together
- Find out how long a period license if valid for
- Have wedding officiator sign license, and send completed form back in

Prepare and Mail Invitations

By now, your invitations should have arrived. Once everything's set, you should send out the invitations no later than six weeks before the wedding. In the case of out-of-town guests, make that at last eight weeks before the wedding. By now, the final guest list should be written "in stone" and you can go about addressing the envelopes. As mentioned earlier, an address which is handwritten or uses calligraphy is the most traditional—and certainly more beautiful and artful.

Make sure that each mailing contains all the right elements—a map and directions, an RSVP card, and a self-addressed stamped, return envelope. Once you are satisfied, go to the post office and send your invitations out.

QUICK NOTES:

- Send out invitations at least six to eight weeks prior to the wedding
- Address envelopes using final guest list
- Addresses are usually handwritten or done in calligraphy
- Double check each mailing for all the proper elements—RSVP card, stamped return envelope, map, etc.

DAY 8—WEB TIPS & RESOURCE GUIDE

Limousines Online

LimousinesOnline.com brings to the Web top a complete Limousine Wedding Registry with a US and Canadian search directory. Once you choose an area, most of the limousine companies listed provide a wedding rate, the minimum number of hours, and the limousine size. If a wedding quote isn't listed, you can request one. A biographical history of listed companies is included, along with a link to those companies that have Web sites.

http://www.limousinesonline.com/weddingregistry/index.html

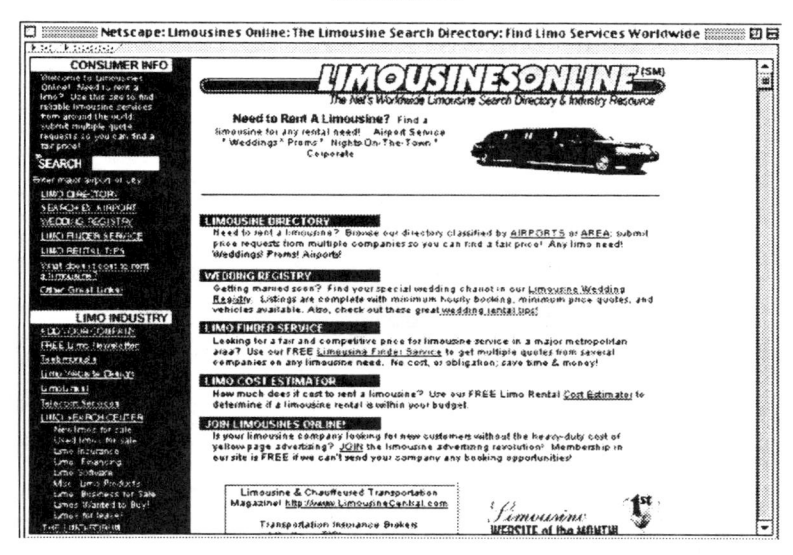

Wednet.com, the all-purpose wedding Web site locates wedding vendors and limos with their regional locator.

http://www.wednet.com/vendors/regionindex.asp

103

Wedding Licenses Online

UltimateWedding.com offers a marriage license guide that does all your homework on wedding licenses from the Web. A geographic locator helps find the county that issues wedding licenses in your area. The Web page for Los Angeles County, for example, gave the following information: Type of licenses available, cost, identification and age requirements, length of time the license remains valid, the number of witnesses needed at the wedding, and the hours, phone number, and location of marriage license offices.

http://www.ultimatewedding.com/legal.htm

In Summary

With the invitations safely on their way, the marriage license in hand, and the limousine waiting in the wings, now is a good time to take a deep breath. Take a moment to think about all the arrangements that you've made thus far. A beautiful day is in the making. Let the steps you'll take next act as sort of a breather, a time to take stock and look at the many details that will *fill in the missing pieces* and create a truly memorable wedding.

Chapter 9

Day 9— Filling in the Missing Pieces

Whether at a wedding or in daily life, it's often all the little things that determine our most cherished memories. The purpose of this planning chapter is to take time to think about wedding details. Do they enhance the overall look and feel of your wedding? Are they unique and special? Do they express your own personal desires?

At this stage in the planning, the reception site should be secured, and the details regarding catering, the number of guests, floral arrangements, and decorations are in place. Still, there are many ways to add charm to the reception. Let's explore some of those now.

Head Table & Decorations

Who sits at the head table? Seating can vary, although traditionally it consists of the bridal party—the maid of honor, best man, bridesmaids, and ushers. If any of these participants are married, you may also decide to include spouses.

Here's another approach to seating the bride and groom that is gaining popularity. Seat the bride and groom at their own, exclusive table. Thus, no one feels left out for not being seated at the head table. Either way, the head table or an exclusive bride and groom's table should stand out with special decorations or flowers.

Four unique ways to make the head table stand out include:

1) Balloons sculptures in the shape of giant hearts or arches can be suspended above the table or from the chairs
2) A special ice sculpture could be placed at either end of the head table—so long as the sight lines to see the bride and groom remain open
3) Use the wedding theme colors with the table linen and a floral arrangement placed at each side of the head table
4) Incorporate candles to create an intimate ambiance

QUICK NOTES:

- Traditionally, the bridal party sits at the head table
- Seat the bride and groom at their own exclusive table
- Dramatize the head table with stylish centerpieces, ice sculptures, large plants or floral arrangements
- Use candles (only if they are permitted and positioned with proper guidance) to add a romantic touch

Reception Table Decorations & Centerpieces

Reception tables can be dressed up with a decorative treatment to enhance the mood. What follows are a dozen ideas for adding a dimension of color and imagination to any reception:

1) A gift basket or heart-shaped box for gift envelopes
2) A wedding wishing well fountain at the entrance
3) Victorian figurine or other unique napkin rings
4) Colored lighting, plus spot lights to illuminate the bride and groom during the first dance, bouquet toss, and toasts.
5) Edible centerpieces made of chocolate or fruit
6) Topiary or other live plants as centerpieces
7) Giant pleated fans or lace along the front of the banquet table
8) Wedding plaque or a commemorative plate with the couple's name on it

9) Framed bride and groom oil portrait or photograph on display.
10) Mementos table, where guests place old photos or other mementos they may have in common with the bride and groom
11) A lighted dance floor
12) Tiny bubbles released from a bubble machine

Party Favors

Party favors offer the opportunity to make an indelible, long-lasting impression. The once popular wedding matchbooks, while still around, now have stiff competition from very creative options, including personalized favors that are useful and practical at the same time. Consider these six unique and personalized alternatives:

1) Chocolate favors with engraved names or wrapped as candy bars are popular
2) Private label wine and champagne—available in per person sizes
3) Christmas ornaments featuring the names of the bride and groom
4) Picture frames that double as guest name cards
5) Perfume, cologne, and body lotions
6) Phone cards with the name of the bride, groom, and wedding date

Reception to-do List

For those who plan their own wedding, it may be helpful to have a friend supervise the pacing of the reception—plus handle any little problems or details that may arise. Some wedding consultants are willing to serve in this capacity by working for *day of the wedding* rates. The advantage of this? It lets the bride and groom enjoy being with guests rather than having to worry about details, such as when to cut the cake or whether to have the band play for an extra half hour.

The following *To-do* checklist will help prepare for many eventualities. All this and more can be discussed in advance with whoever you appoint or hire as a coordinator or consultant. This will help things run smoothly.

RECEPTION TO-DO CHECKLIST

- Total # Tables:
- # Centerpieces:
- # Party Favors:
- # Disposable Cameras for tables
- Head Table Decorations:
- Order Decorations/Centerpieces/Favors
- Confirm All Delivery/Pick-up Dates
- Special Table/Decorations
- Special Tables/Fountains
- Make list of announcements for Emcee/DJ
- Make a list of toast makers for Emcee/DJ
- Write Bride/Groom statement or announcement
- Special knife for cake cutting
- Choose "first dance" song, special dances for band/DJ
- Guest book, pen, and floral decoration
- Place Cards
- Bouquet toss
- Garter toss
- Appoint a reception supervisor/coordinator to help with these details before, during, and after the wedding
- Discuss overtime arrangements and decisions regarding music, photography, and site should wedding go longer than expected

Make the Seating Plan

Many weddings place guests at pre-arranged tables. Look at your final guest list and place together those guests who have a basis for sharing the same table. This can be based on family, friends, age range, common interests, and a whole range of criteria. This is the match-making part of your job, and it can enhance your guest's enjoyment and experience. You could, for example, place all newly-wedded couples together at the same table (They certainly have a lot in common)!

Another option, is a la carte seating—in other words, let everyone choose their own seats. We did this at our own wedding, and amazingly enough, the right people sat next to each other! Had we drawn up a table seating chart, it would have been nearly identical to the choices our guests made.

DAY 9—WEB TIPS & RESOURCE GUIDE

Reception Decorations and Party Favors Online

The Web is a great place to find and shop for personalized products. Most of the all-purpose wedding Web sites make finding party favors and decorations easy. Here are two that we've mentioned before.

http://wedding-world.com/favors.html
http://www.wednet.com/vendors/regionindex.asp

TheWeddingShopper.com carries everything from picture frame place cards and satin roses to personalized Christmas ornaments and chocolate candy bars. And, they feature items from many quality, name brand manufacturers, such as Beverly Clark.

http://www.theweddingshopper.com

(see picture next page)

Personalize.com offers a very nice, quality selection of wedding favors, as well as bridal accessories such as garters, personalized handkerchiefs, and Unity candles.

http://www.personalize.com

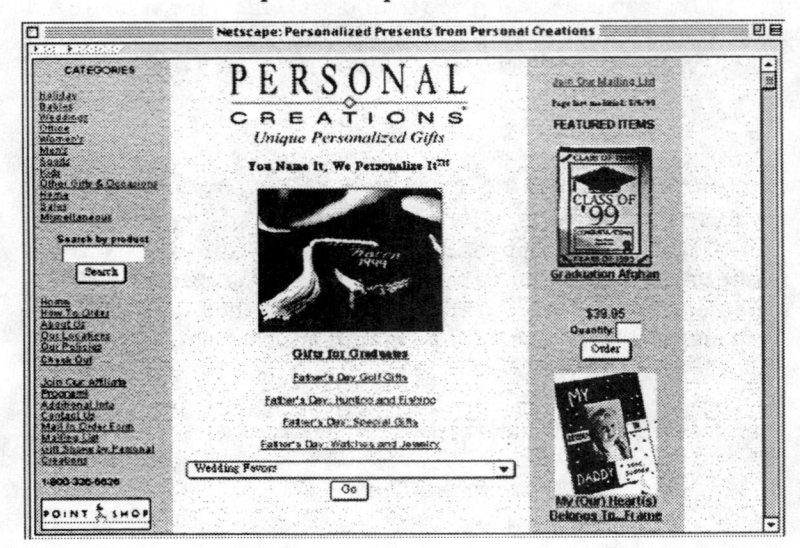

In Summary

By attending to all the details, you have—like the most successful artist—filled in all the details of your wonderful painting and left nothing to chance. Much of the planning work is behind you. Some of your next planning days will deal with the confirming *facts and fun* for both the wedding and the honeymoon.

Chapter 10

Day 10— Checking in for Facts & Fun

Welcome to a planning theme worth waiting for. Confirming with vendors is relatively easy, and you can do most of it on the phone. Make it even easier by sharing this task with your significant other-to-be. Now that the wedding planning is in the home stretch, teamwork really helps.

Confirm Wedding Sites & Vendors

If you are already organized, then this should be a snap. You've probably spoken with your wedding vendors several times, but now with about one month to go before the wedding, it's time to call again. What will you discuss? Basically, you'll want to confirm what you've already agreed upon, as well as get or give updates on any additional information that is relevant. For example, you might give the DJ or band leader an updated song list. Or, you might tell the caterer about a last minute change. The important thing is to be as thorough as possible.

Go to your wedding organizer/folder and look at all the vendors with whom you've made arrangements. Start at the beginning and have all your most recent notes handy.

CONFIRMATION CHECKLIST

VENDORS
- Clergy/Rabbi/Officiator
- Ceremony Site Manager
- Reception Site Manager
- Caterer/Banquet Manager
- Hotel Accommodations
- Bridal Gown Vendor
- Bridal Accessories Vendor
- Tuxedo Shop
- Hairdresser/Manicurist/Make-up
- Band Leader/DJ/Emcee
- Photographer
- Videographer
- Limousine Company
- Florist
- Bridal Party
- Wedding License
- Reception Decorations Vendors

RSVP Time

Eventually, those RSVPs will start returning, and you'll be able to track your guest count. Find out when your caterer needs a final count (for ordering the right quantity of food).

Guests who don't reply in time for this final count will have to be called. Be patient, polite, and understanding for those who don't reply right away. Remember that even when you get your final count, your caterer should have some leeway for extra guests or others who may arrive.

Plan the Honeymoon Trip

Of all the trips you take, none will have the anticipation of the honeymoon trip. You now have the bragging rights to let everyone know this is your honeymoon. It only happens once, so make the most of it by planning a trip that both of you can cherish forever. The honeymoon was not included in the budget for a reason. We didn't want you to start limiting or prioritizing this one-of-a-kind trip. If you have stayed within your budget, you will know what you can afford to spend on the honeymoon. You might even be lucky enough to have relatives who give you a week at their time-share resort. Or, perhaps a flight attendant in the family will offer to give you two complimentary airline tickets as a wedding gift. Always plan far enough in advance so that you can take time off of work.

You may decide to speak with a travel agent to put your trip together. Or, as you'll soon find, you can arrange your entire trip—including tours of all kinds—over the Internet. One of the best ways to plan a successful trip is to communicate about what you like and don't like. How do you want to spend your honeymoon? Do you want to sight-see in a country or exotic place where neither of you have ever been? Or do you want to talk long walks on the beach and just unwind? Or maybe a little of both? After you've narrowed down what you want to do, you can begin to search out where you'd like to go.

Next, you'll have to decide when you want to leave. You might opt to leave the night of, or the day after the wedding. If so, expect to be tired. Another idea is to give yourself two or three days after the wedding before leaving for the honeymoon. This will give you enough time to say goodbye to friends and family, and to tie up some loose ends—as well as get a moment's rest—before leaving on your trip. It will also allow you to open the gifts—and record who gave you what gift. If you do this now, completing the *Thank You* notes later on will be a little easier.

Again, don't be shy about telling people you've just gotten married. Others will join in the glow of your recent union. You may get some preferential treatment, such as complimentary wine or champagne on your airplane flight, an upgraded room at the hotel, and so on. Besides, you've earned the bragging rights! So enjoy.

QUICK NOTES:

- Plan far enough in advance to take off work
- Communicate about what kind of honeymoon trip you want—such as sight-seeing in an exotic setting or relaxing on a sunny beach
- If possible, wait a day or two before leaving
- Let travel agents and others know that you are honeymooning

DAY 10—WEB TIPS & RESOURCE GUIDE

Honeymoon Planning Online

Just about everything you can think of to plan your honeymoon trip can be done online—maybe even more than what you dreamed was possible. Here's a sampling of how you can plan and prepare for all aspects of your trip—whether it's a nonstop adventure or a soothing sensual pleasure.

Where to Go

The CIA's World Factbook is a great Web site for honeymooners who want to gather a wide range of information about the countries they'll be visiting—especially the more exotic ones. This site includes each nation's customs, religions, languages, capital, type of legal system, primary industries, type of currency, exchange rate, and more. You'll even find out about national holidays, in case you do or don't want to be surprised. You may even find about naturally occurring hazards and environmental issues such as earthquake and hurricane zones.

http://www.odci.gov/cia/publications/factbook/index.html

(see picture next page)

The Tourism Offices Worldwide Web site lets you search thousands of tourism offices in the US and other Countries.

http://www.mbnet.mb.ca/lucas/travel/tourism-offices.html

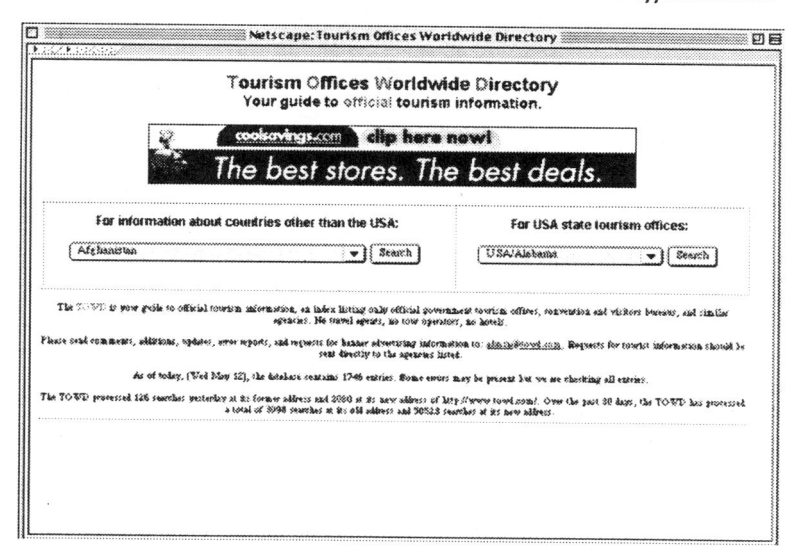

Want to plan a surprise trip to a music event or concert during your honeymoon? Culturefinder.com offers a convenient way to get tickets for music, opera, dance, and other art events in cities throughout the US. It's located at:

http://www.culturefinder.com

Innsite.com offers a complete Internet directory of bed and breakfasts throughout the US and internationally. In all, over 12,000 pages of bed and breakfast establishments are indexed!

http://www.innsite.com

Travel Arrangements Online

Microsoft Network, a.k.a. MSN, hosts Expedia, a popular site that lets you compare prices—even check for the best fares. The site requires no password, and it features useful maps and trip-planning tools and accessories. If you're looking for cruises, resorts, and vacation packages, this site might be the place to go.

http://www.expedia.msn.com/daily/home/default.hts
(see picture next page)

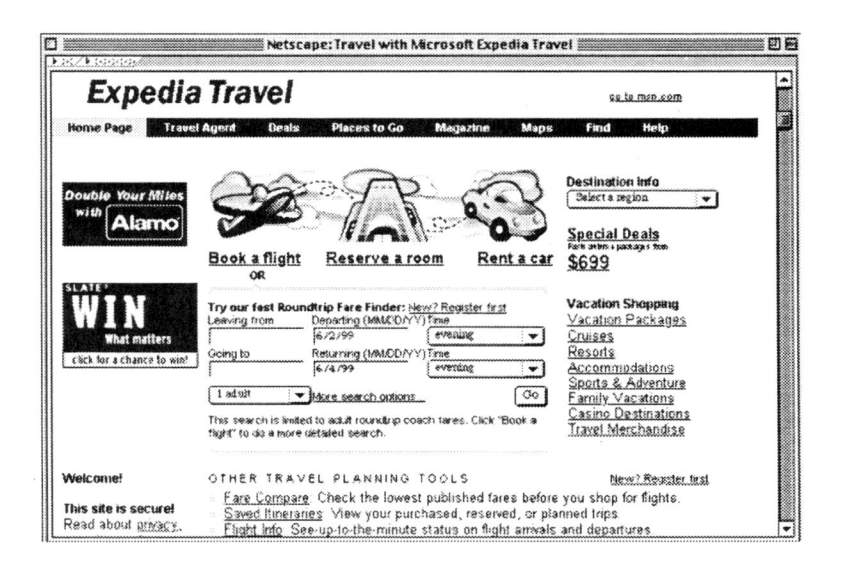

Then there are all-purpose travel sites. These often feature methods for planning the trip, finding the lowest fares, and reserving hotel accommodations. You can also expect to find useful travel tools, such as a currency converter, destination guides, and detailed maps for states and cities maps. Here are some comprehensive, highly visited sites:

http://www.trip.com
http://www.priceline.com
http://www.cheaptickets.com
http:www.travelocity.com
http://www.bestfares.com
http://www.luxurylink.com
http:www.ebay.com

Travel publishers like Fodor's and Frommer's also have web sites worth checking out. Fodor's features a Hotel and Restaurant Index; Frommer's offers Budget Travel Online.

http://www.fodors.com
http://www.frommers.com

Weather Reports Online

WorldClimate.com can be used to check the weather in your honeymoon destination. Want to know if your honeymoon trip to Paris is likely to be rainy? You'll find the average monthly temperature and rainfall for thousands of cities, regions, and countries worldwide.

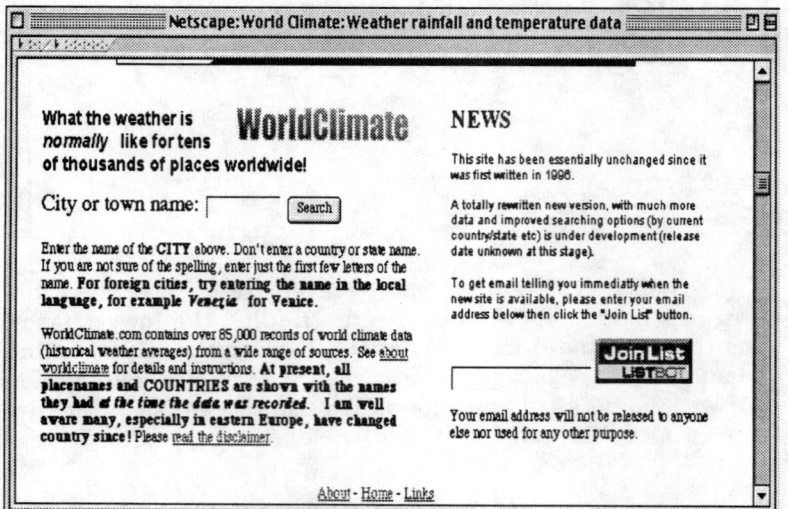

http://www.worldclimate.com

Another site, Intellicast.com, offers up-to-date weather forecasts for the United States and the world. It's especially helpful if you're honeymooning in the USA because of its monthly weather patterns for 12 different United States' regions.

http://www.intellicast.com

In Summary

Now that the wedding services are confirmed and the honeymoon is planned, you can anticipate the wedding and honeymoon with confidence and excitement. The next planning day theme will let you explore how to put the *personalized touch* on some final details.

Chapter 11

Day 11— The Personalized Touch

Personal memories are among life's true treasures. This chapter's theme—with tasks that take about a day to complete—are about making the most of memories, and about showing appreciation to those who have accepted a role in your wedding. Let's explore a few ways to accomplish these worthwhile goals.

Buy the Guest Book & Pen

By now, you have undoubtedly come across your share of guest books. The guest book is the first thing people notice when they enter the reception. Try to have a special guest signing table set aside for this purpose. Adorn the table with a lace tablecloth, a floral arrangement, or other decorations. Another possibility? Use a candle to dress up the table—but always take precautions against the possibility of fire since some children may also want to sign the guest book. This might require stationing an usher at the sign-in table.

Purchase a guest book, or adapt a personal diary into one. Unique diaries, which make beautiful guest books, can be found in boutique shops and stationery stores. For a writing instrument, think about something stylish and special. A fountain pen or glass pen, for example, can be used in conjunction with any number of inks. Try out the pen to make sure it's easy to use, and that it's not too messy. For this reason, water soluble ink is a good idea. If possible, assign a friend or usher to stand by the table and invite all the guests to sign-in. This helps should the entrance become crowded, thus making it difficult for guests to see the sign-in book.

QUICK NOTES:

- Make a special guest sign-in table
- Adorn the table with lace, flowers, or other decorations
- Consider an elegant fountain pen or glass writing instrument
- Have an usher at the table to invite guests to sign-in

Purchase Personalized Gifts for Wedding Party

With so many details needing attention, it's easy for something like wedding party gifts to slip through the cracks. By planning early, however, you'll save yourself some stress when wedding crunch time rapidly approaches. Engraving gifts can take time, so order at least two weeks or more in advance to guarantee that the gifts are ready when you need them.

Should all women's gifts and all men's gifts be the same? By all means, no—in fact, gifts for the maid of honor and the best man may be different and more expensive than those given to other bridal party members. Bridesmaids gifts can be identical, as can all the gifts for ushers. Actually, these won't really be identical because they will be engraved with the initials or name of the recipient. Because these individuals are close friends and family, make sure that the gift you select means something to the one who receives it. If desired, personalized gifts can also be given to the fathers and mothers of the bride and groom.

QUICK NOTES:

- Engraving takes time, so order gifts at least two weeks in advance of presentation
- If desired, give unique gifts to the maid of honor and the best man

- Get all gifts engraved with initials or name
- Personalized gifts can also be given to the parents of the bride and groom

DAY 11—WEB TIPS & RESOURCE GUIDE

Guest Books & Personalized Wedding Gifts Online

Looking for the perfect guest book? Or do you hope to find the one personalized item that you know your Best Man or Maid of Honor would love? Use the Web Yellow Pages to find local establishments—even those located right down the street.

Or, use all-purpose wedding Web sites and specialized gift sites like those below. Be prepared to be astounded at the variety of gifts available—from imported wedding handkerchiefs and engraved blown glass to personalized, hand-painted gifts:

http://www.wednet.com/vendors/regionindex.asp
http://wedding-world.com/gifts.html
http://www.weddinghankies.com
http://www.911gifts.com

Lastly, Personalize.com features a large selection of personalized wedding gifts for the Maid of Honor and bridesmaids, including jewelry, keepsake boxes, and picture frames. For the Best Man and ushers there are personalized cherry wood humidors, heirloom pocket watches, and engraved rose wood pens.

http://www.personalize.com

In Summary

The planning work you have just completed will provide heartfelt feelings all around. You've accomplished one other feat—you have completed most of your wedding purchases, both large and small (with the exception of the rehearsal dinner). And if you've stayed on budget, you deserve an extra pat on the back! Now, with your wedding day only weeks—or days away and counting—it's time to start *preparing for things to come*.

Chapter 12

Day 12— Preparing for Things to Come

The rehearsal dinner is a celebration that brings all your bridal party and family together—maybe for the first time. You'll want to plan this special occasion with as much care as all the other phases of your wedding.

Coordinate the Rehearsal Dinner
The rehearsal dinner is a time to have fun and be at ease. Here is more than an opportunity to introduce future in-laws and out-of-towners to each other (that is, assuming they haven't already met). This is the last time all participants will be together to ask questions, understand their roles and responsibilities, and practice the ceremony together. If it's in your budget, have the photographer and videographer take pictures of the rehearsal dinner.

Where should the rehearsal dinner take place? It can be held in the home or at a restaurant. If you decide to meet at a restaurant, be sure to reserve in advance. For large parties, some restaurants require booking through the restaurant manager or booking agent. Because this could require a slightly longer lead time, err on the safe side and make rehearsal reservations at least one, even two weeks in advance. This will increase the likelihood of getting a private room or semi-private area in the restaurant.

Afterwards, the rehearsal itself may take place at the actual site, or wherever the officiant can lead the group through the rehearsal practice. This normally includes the processional order, readings, blocking of the bridal party, the recessional, and anything else that needs practice. Should you have a wedding program, give everyone a copy to use as a guide. And, if possible, use the actual music for the rehearsal.

How long should the rehearsal practice be? Take as many practice walk-throughs as are necessary, but don't overdo it. Basically, the practice session should continue until everyone understands what to do. When the rehearsal is over, give instructions for everyone to arrive at the ceremony site fully dressed no less than an hour before the scheduled ceremony.

QUICK NOTES:

- Hold rehearsal dinner at home or at a favorite restaurant
- For larger parties, book reservations in advance
- If in the budget, have the photographer take pictures
- Use actual music and the wedding program as guide
- Take as many walk-throughs as needed
- Ask everyone to arrive fully dressed, one hour before ceremony

Attendant Briefings

You may want to make a list of those activities and jobs that are entrusted to the Maid of Honor and Best Man. What are these? Well, for the Maid of Honor, duties could include: Helping the bride meet all appointments for hair and make-up, carrying the groom's wedding band, and assisting the bride with her gown's train, veil, and other accessories. The Best Man's duties often include: Paying the officiator on behalf of the bride and groom, keeping track of the marriage license and travel itinerary, carrying the bride's ring, toasting the newlyweds, and transporting gifts from the reception to the newlywed's home. And of course, both can act as witnesses on the marriage license.

Others, such as ushers, can assist in seating, handing out programs, and tending the guest-book. Try to give everyone involved something to do.

Remember, too, that there are some after-the-wedding tasks that close friends can help with, such as returning the tux, cleaning the gown, preserving the bridal bouquet, and driving you to the airport for the departing honeymoon flight. By providing a list, you'll be making their job that much easier—and there won't be any mix-ups about what you need.

QUICK NOTES:

- Write down a list of activities that you need the Maid of Honor, the Best Man, and any others to help you with
- For Maid of Honor: Drive bride to hair and make-up appointments, carry groom's band, assist with bridal gown and accessories during ceremony, bring gown for cleaning, and send bouquet for preservation after the wedding
- For Best Man: Carry bride's ring, pay wedding officiator, keep track of documents like travel itinerary and marriage license, make a reception toast, transport gifts from reception to newlywed's home, return tux, and drive newlyweds to airport after the wedding

Pack for the Honeymoon

Packing for the honeymoon shouldn't be too hard—should it? We hope not, but after all you've been through, if you wait until after the wedding you may too happily dazed and tired to pack like you normally might. So try to pack in advance, even if it's two or three days before. This will put one more job behind you. If you have time, check the newspaper for weather conditions to determine if you need to pack that umbrella, sweater, or thick socks. Don't forget to bring all your maps, guides, and of course, a working camera to chronicle your honeymoon.

One final tip? Try to pack light—that way you'll be able to easily bring back honeymoon souvenirs.

DAY 12—WEB TIPS & RESOURCE GUIDE

Rehearsal Dinner Locations Online

Looking for places to have your rehearsal dinner? Naturally, you can use the Web Yellow Pages to find local restaurants. If you haven't book marked these as favorite Web pages you might want to do so.

http://yp.yahoo.com/
http://yellowpages.zip2.com/
http://yp.superpages.com/

Honeymoon Travel Preparation Online

To make your honeymoon trip as comfortable as possible, we've reprised two useful Web sites here (see Chapter 10 for a more complete list of travel-related sites):

Trip.com is an all-purpose travel site. It includes a trip planner that locates pricing and accommodations. It also features useful travel tools, including a currency converter, destination guides, and detailed maps for states and cities maps.

http://www.trip.com

Intellicast.com offers up-to-date weather forecasts for the United States and the world. It's especially helpful if you're honeymooning in the USA because of its monthly weather patterns for 12 different United States' regions.

http://www.intellicast.com

In Summary

With the rehearsal dinner planned, you're just about at the finish line. In this final planning theme before the wedding, you'll check every last thing as you *countdown to the special day*.

Chapter 13

Day 13— Countdown to the Special Day

With the wedding only days away, you need to constantly check and recheck the preparations. This includes going through the final checklist and bringing all miscellaneous items together. You don't, for example, want to realize five minutes before the ceremony begins that the wine glasses used in your ceremony are missing. Or, worse, maybe even the wine!

Gather All Miscellaneous Items

The time to review the final checklist is before the rehearsal dinner. This will help identify anything that has slipped past. Even apparently minor things—like how to light the candles during the ceremony—need to addressed. (Lighting the candles, for example, is most elegantly done by using a handheld, switch activated butane lighter, not matches.) Write down all the details for the ceremony and reception, and go through the checklist to make sure that every item, no matter how small, is present and accounted for.

FINAL CHECKLIST

CEREMONY

- Bridal Attire: Gown and all accessories
- Groom Attire: Tux and all accessories

- Confirm Hair, Make-up, Manicure
- Bouquets, Corsages, Boutonnieres, (Have someone bring these to the ceremony 1 hour in advance)
- Unity Candle/Candles
- Special Decorated Tables (for candles, readings, etc.)
- Butane Lighter for candle
- Rice or Bird seed
- Limousine Confirmed
- Hair dresser/Manicurist/Make-up
- Band Leader/DJ/Emcee
- Photographer
- Videographer
- Limousine time and location confirmed
- Wedding Programs
- Wedding License
- Music cassettes, CDs
- Wedding Rings
- Wine Glasses/Wine/Other ceremony necessities
- Bridal Party Gifts
- Transportation for Parents, Groom
- Flower girl Basket/flowers
- Ring Pillow
- Ceremony Runner
- All other Decorations for Ceremony
- Reception Line, traditionally ordered as follows:
    Mother of Bride
    Father and Mother of Groom
    Father of Bride
    Bride and Groom
    Maid of Honor and bridesmaids.
- Wedding Party & Formal Photography

RECEPTION
- Make Final Payments for:
    - Caterer
    - Musicians
    - Photographer & Videographer
    - Limousine Chauffeur
    - Bartender
    - Other Vendors
- Guest book, pen, and table decorations
- Table numbers, Place Cards
- Cake Table, Special Cake Knife
- Cake Topper/Flowers
- Party Favors
- Flowers and plants
- Centerpieces
- Candles
- All Reception Decorations, extras
- Disposable Cameras
- Special table linens, napkin rings, etc
- Gift Table Set-up
- Cocktails/Open Bar
- Bride and Groom Entrance/Introduction by Emcee/DJ
- Champagne Glasses
- Toasting
- Wedding Dance Songs
- Bouquet Toss
- Garter Toss
- Signed Wedding License

HONEYMOON & AFTER WEDDING
- Transport Gifts Back Home
- Make a Record of Gifts
- Check packing and all documents
- Travel maps, weather, and Itinerary
- Tickets
- Emergency phone numbers
- Travelers Checks/Currency
- Passports
- Ride to Airport
- Return Tux to Tuxedo Shop
- Preserve Gown/Bridal Bouquet
- Mail out completed wedding license

DAY 13—WEB TIPS & RESOURCE GUIDE

Online Checklist

Remember back to when you first created a Web wedding calendar and checklist? Well, if that is where you have stored your wedding information, take a look at your master list. Print it out, or create a new one with the items listed above at one of these free Web calendar sites:

http://www.calendar.yahoo.com
http://www.visto.com
http://www.magicaldesk.com
http://www.scheduleonline.com
http://www.pacificawebcal.net

Web home pages from two more calendar sites are shown on the next page.

http://www.jump.com

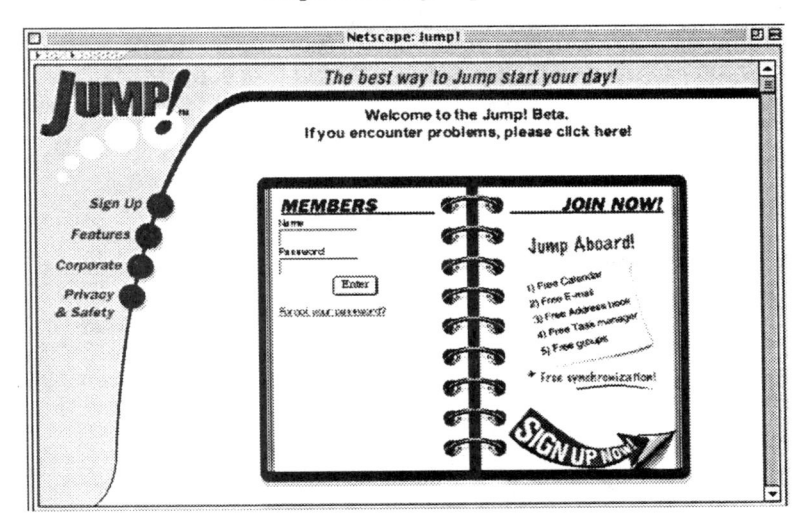

http://www.when.com

In Summary

Having packed and gone through your final checklist, there's only one thing left to do—get married. So try to get a good night's sleep before your special day. In the next chapter, you'll be planning for your *new beginning*. So, congratulations!

Chapter 14

Day 14— Wrapping Up for a New Beginning

This last planning "day" is essentially a successful conclusion to all that you've done to bring your beautiful wedding day to fruition. Now comes time for tying up the loose ends. If you've moved, for example, you'll need to send out moving announcements. Best of all, there's no more pressure. The point of these last remaining tasks is to preserve your cherished memories for a long time to come.

Preserve the Wedding Gown & Bouquet

By the time you return from the honeymoon, the tuxedo should have been returned. Now, you may want to find a shop that can clean and box the gown for preservation. You may also decide to preserve the bridal bouquet in some kind of keepsake arrangement. Use the Internet Yellow Pages to find a floral preservation specialist.

Write Thank You Notes

The easiest and most efficient way to write thank you notes is to keep good records. Early on, for example, you will probably receive some envelopes with checks enclosed. Make it a habit to go to your guest list and immediately write in the amount of the gift. Actually, you're doing much more than keeping good records, you're doing some important work up front that will save time and enhance accuracy later on. Do the same upon opening any gifts—even if you open them the night of the reception or the next morning. Don't wait too long before writing everything down, because once cards get separated from the gifts, you'll find it difficult to match the right name with the right gift

When should you send your notes? Some etiquette books state that thank you notes should be sent up to six months or more after the wedding. However, why not send them out as soon as possible after returning from the honeymoon? Until the notes are sent, guests will wonder whether or not you got their gift. So, if possible, wait no longer than three months before sending out your thank you notes.

Should thank you notes be personalized? A personalized note will mean much more to someone who went to the trouble of picking out a gift just for you. This may take time, so work as a team to figure out what to say. Mention the gift by name, even saying where or how you intend to use it. The note can be signed by either one or both of you. And, if you've already gotten your wedding album and extra prints, you might want to include a specially chosen photograph from the wedding.

QUICK NOTES:

- Record gifts and checks the same day they arrive
- Don't let gifts and cards get separated
- Personalize thank you notes
- Include a special photo, if desired

DAY 14—WEB TIPS & RESOURCE GUIDE

Bridal Gown Preservation Online

WedGown.com is the Web site for Imperial Gown, which offers a gown preservation service.

www.wedgown.com

(see picture next page)

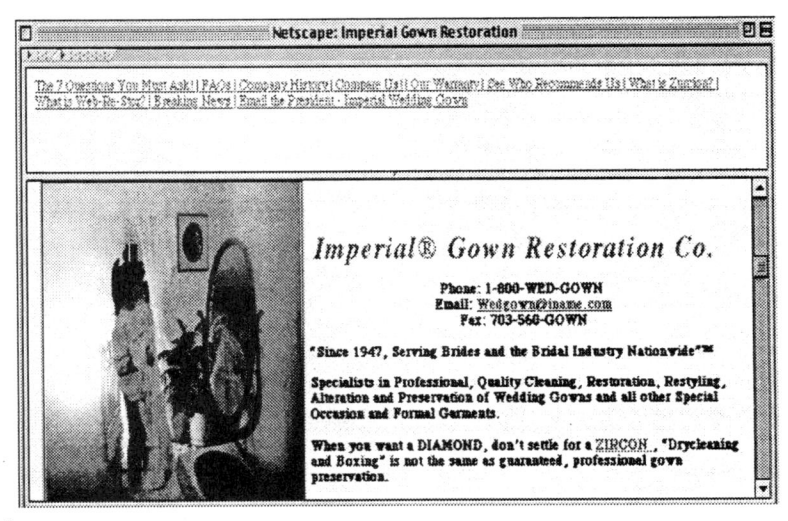

Bridal Bouquet Preservation Online

As mentioned in Chapter 7, here are some bridal preservation Web sites that will create floral keepsakes.

Forever Yours Keepsakes, Ltd. preserves those one-of-a-kind bridal and other floral arrangements.

http://www.westnet.com/fyk

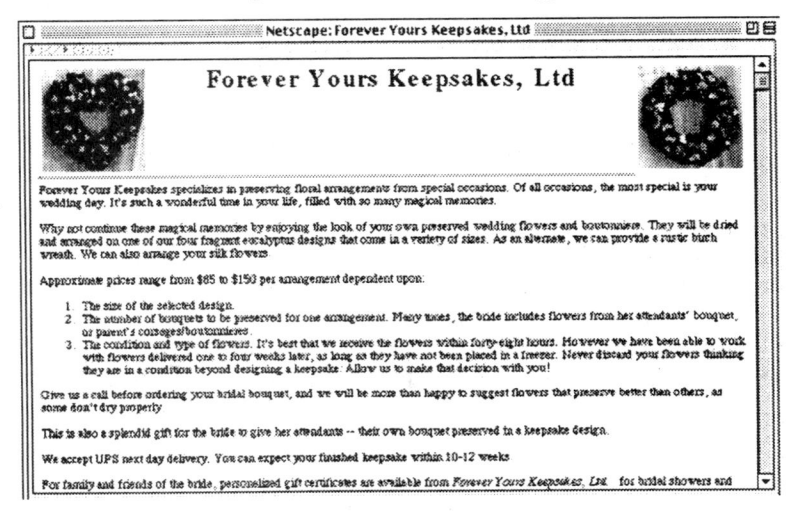

Blooming-color.com carefully presses each flower, then preserves bouquets in their original shape. They will even preserve the boutonniere with in a "bridal flower picture."

http://blooming-color.com

Paula's Petals is a company that specializes in freeze drying flowers and bouquets. They create displays—that can include the invitation or other memento—in a variety of shadow boxes, and can even replace damaged flowers.

http://www.paulaptl.qpg.com

In Summary
Congratulations on having completed one of life's most significant events! We hope that this book has been a useful companion during your wedding planning. May you be blessed with the same preparation, passion, compassion, and patience for realizing all of your life goals and dreams.

Index

A
announcements, 26-27
attendants, 126

B
beverages, 54-55
bridal registry, 42-43
   department store, 48
   online, 46-48
   specialty, 48
budget, 8-13
   checklist, 11-13

C
cake, 58
   checklist, 59
calendar, 5
   web, 16-18
candle lighting, 64
cards, 69
catering, 30, 51-54
   budget tips, 55-57
   checklist, 53-54
centerpiece, 106
ceremony, 63-66
   checklist, 65-66
ceremony site, 27-28
chamber of commerce, 34
clergy, 25, 64
confirmation, 113
   checklist, 114
credit cards, 10

D
dessert reception, 56
DJ, 67-68, 71-73

E
English High Tea, 57
etiquette, 64

F
favors, 107
flowers, 87-88
   preservation, 89

F (cont.)
   checklist, 89-90
   final checklist, 129-132
   formal, 9

G
gifts
   wedding party, 122
   gowns, 38-41
   antique, 39
   designer, 39-40
   fitting, 92
   rental, 41
gowns, 38-41
   preservation, 135
guest book, 121
guest list, 24-25

H
head table, 105-106
   decorations, 106
honeymoon, 115-116
   packing, 127
hotels, 82-83

I
invitations, 66-70
   checklist, 70
   mailing, 102

L
limousine, 99
   checklist, 100-101

M
maps, 74
music, 66-68
   checklist, 68
   online, 71-73

O
officiator, 25-26, 63
online
   announcements, 32

O (cont.)

online (cont.)
- budgeting, 14-15
- calendars 16-18, 133
- catering, 60-62
- chamber of commerce, 34-35
- DJ, 71-73
- etiquette, 21
- favors, 109
- financial tools, 15-16
- flowers, 92-94
  - preservation, 135
- gifts, 123-124
- gowns, 43-45
  - preservation, 136
- hotels, 84
- honeymoon, 116-120, 128
- invitations, 73-74
- limousine, 103
- maps, 74
- music, 71-73
- photography, 83
- reception sites, 33-34
- registries, 46-48
- rehearsal dinner, 128
- travel, 118-119
- tuxedo, 95-97
- videography, 83
- weather, 119-120
- wedding license, 104
- wedding rings, 45-46
- wedding sites, 18-21, 44-45

P

photography, 77-79
- checklist, 79

Post, Emily, 64

printing
- engraved, 69
- thermographic, 69

P (cont.)

priorities, 6-7
- checklist, 7

processional, 64

R

rabbi, 25
reading, 64
reception, 31
- checklist, 107-108
- registry, 42-42
rehearsal dinner, 125
rings, 42
RSVP, 69, 102, 114

S

seating, 109
semi-formal, 9
sites, 27-31
- ceremony, 27-28
- checklist, 30-31
- reception, 28-30

T

thank you notes, 135-136
tuxedo, 90
- checklist, 91

V

Valentine's Day, 5
Victorian, 9
videography, 80-82
vows, 64

W

wedding
- calendar, 5
- license, 101-102
- program, 64
- theme, 9
wedding party, 23, 65

Y

Yellow Pages
- Internet, 60-62